pig boy's wicked bird

A MEMOIR

Doug Crandell

CHICAGO
REVIEW
PRESS

Library of Congress Cataloging-in-Publication Data

Crandell, Doug.

Pig Boy's wicked bird : a memoir / Doug Crandell.— 1st ed.

p.   cm.

ISBN 1-55652-552-4

1. Crandell, Doug—Childhood and youth. 2. Crandell, Doug—Homes and haunts—Indiana—Wabash Region. 3. Wabash Region (Ind.)—Social life and customs. 4. Authors, American—21st century—Biography. 5. Rural families—Indiana—Wabash Region. 6. Accident victims—Indiana—Biography. 7. Farm life—Indiana—Wabash Region. 8. Fingers—Wounds and injuries. I. Title.

PS3603.R377Z47 2004

818'.603—dc22   2004003530

For the other 6 D's,
who taught me how to use work for healing

Jacket photo: *Piglet Hindquarters* © Corbis

Jacket and interior design: Laura Lindgren

First edition

Published by Chicago Review Press, Incorporated

814 North Franklin Street

Chicago, Illinois 60610

ISBN 1-55652-552-4

Printed in the United States of America

5 4 3 2 1

"If I could do it, I'd do no writing at all here. It would be photographs; the rest would be fragments of cloth, bits of cotton, lumps of earth, records of speech, pieces of wood and iron, phials of odors, plates of food and of excrement.... A piece of the body torn out by the root might be more to the point."

—JAMES AGEE, 1941

* * *

" 'Cause they told me, when I was younger, boy you're gonna be
    President,
But just like everything else those crazy dreams just kinda came
    and went,
But ain't that America for you and me, Ain't that America,
    something to see baby."

—JOHN MELLENCAMP, 1984

The adults around the boy didn't understand his weight gain; they couldn't figure out how the toddler had put on extra pounds when he hadn't been eating. He appeared to be bulging under his pleated shorts, his tummy full and plump. He was a farm child, and at first the grown-ups thought he might have the worms, what with the way his belly arched, but they quickly determined this was not the case. He was extremely healthy in every regard: bright eyes, hair luminous, stomach not merely distended with air but pudgy, like a working man's. Yet the boy hadn't been eating lately. He wouldn't touch the sausage and corn pones at breakfast, or the ham and eggs at lunch, or the flavorful evening meal of stew, beans, more cornbread, and slices of thick cheese. They were perplexed: how was the child becoming fuller and fuller, skin smooth and perfect, his little hands chubby and nails pink, with fine half-moons of white near the quick?

One day, after the men and older boys had gone to the fields, the grandmother (or was it the mother? an aunt? perhaps a female friend of the family?) decided to follow the little guy wherever he went. It was a family farm, and not much thought was given to allowing a child to roam around unattended to explore the pasture or play in the corn. Most of the adults simply thought it safe for children to be children and let the young ones play until they got hungry and came looking for food. But this boy had not been coming back to the house for his meals. The woman was determined to find out why.

At first, the little boy merely sat in the tall grass of the pasture, where he played with butterflies and plucked grass to chew. The woman watched him from behind a tree. She knew the grass could not be putting on the little boy's pounds and certainly wouldn't keep him from eating at regular meals. Before long the child became bored and got to his feet. He waddled down a worn hog path to the side entrance of the farrowing house. The spring had been plentiful in terms of newborn piglets; the building held more than ten litters. The sows were all seasoned matrons; they were well mannered and docile, good mothers and even better livestock.

The woman watched through the door of the shed as the little boy strode down the aisle where the sows lay on their sides grunting, urging their piglets to quit running around in chase and come to nurse. The woman closed her eyes for a minute, trying to keep herself from thinking of what she knew she'd see when she opened them.

The boy struggled over a plank separating the stall from the aisle. He managed to pull his weight over the partition; the woman thought for sure that she heard his tight little shorts rip. She opened her eyes. The fat baby boy was down on his round belly suckling from a crossbred sow. The other little pigs, his siblings, squealed to get him to move over so that they might find a teat; the sow perked her ears at this commotion but remained flat on her side, underbelly splayed wide so that her young could easily nurse.

The little boy seemed to doze off as he drank from the sow's nipple. The woman was shocked but oddly relieved. The boy would have to be stopped, of course, but at least he didn't have some dreadful disease that made him look healthy while inside he invisibly starved to death. On the farm, only cow's milk was used for human beings, and the woman knew, from bottle-feeding piglets that had lost their mothers during birthing, that sow's milk was bitter, almost sour tasting. She wondered how on earth the child had ever gotten used to the taste, but instantly, seeing the boy nursing, she could understand how he might've thought this was simply natural. After all, there were more pigs around him than humans, and both he and the piglets were roughly in the same developmental stage, so it made sense to her that the little boy thought what he was doing was normal, even proper and right.

The woman waited until the little boy had fallen completely asleep. She opened the shed door quietly and walked to the stall where he lay deeply dreaming. She had to position herself just right, maneuvering over the partition to lift the heavy child from the pile of piglets that had crowded around him for warmth. The woman struggled to pull the full child to her bosom and strained to cradle his bulk as she toted him to the house. Once she got him inside, and he woke up, she would tell him how he was not to do what he'd been doing, how it wasn't clean and that God made mommy sows for baby pigs and regular mommies for baby boys and girls. But for now she'd let him sleep, his blond, sweaty bangs clinging to his forehead, the scent of sharp milk on his hot breath as he breathed in and out like a little piglet.

PART I

Who Is the Real Pig Boy?

When I mentioned the Pig Boy story to my father, he seemed puzzled at first. "No," he said blandly, "I don't remember anyone telling that."

I pushed him a little further. "You know, the adults didn't understand how the little kid was getting fatter but not eating?" He became animated, moved his hands like he was taking a livestock bid; an auctioneer, he's never lost the showmanship of the ring.

"I believe I do remember that. Yes. But I am not sure who that was." He hanged his head a little. Was it something to be ashamed of? I know *I've* certainly not told many people the story. Did he know something I didn't?

"Was it you?" I asked, half joking, but wanting it to be him, to get off the hook myself.

"No," he quickly responded. He peered past me, over my shoulder, to a movie of memory that apparently was playing on the wall behind me.

He stopped staring and turned to me. "Maybe it was you," he

said, smiling, the look in his tired eyes saying he knew the whole truth and nothing but the truth. I dropped the subject and asked how his knees were doing, thoughts of Pig Boy running rampant in my head as spooked livestock.

I do hope so very badly that it wasn't me. But the thing is, I was chunky too, and picky about food. If that was it, I might not even wonder if I could have been the pig boy, but another distinct memory of my maternal grandparents and their house in Terre Haute, Indiana, haunts me. In their living room was a Bible that stood a half-foot thick when closed. It was white with gold lettering on the cover, silver filigreed on every page, and color pictures of the Crucifixion, and I coveted the thing, wanted to steal it, but knew that would mean my untimely damnation to Hell.

On that same table was a pewter statue of Romulus and Remus nursing at the drooping breasts of a strong she-wolf. The brothers were knelt down on either side of their wild mother. I'd stare at that statue for what seemed like days, taking it all in, trying to understand what the boys were doing to the animal, how it was that she could mother something that was not like her. I'd trail my fingers along the tarnished metal and put them to my nose to smell. Somehow, I'd gotten the idea that the statue was part of the same biblical motif that my grandparents adorned their home with, sacred and holy. When I recall the table with the Bible and statue, I close my eyes and try hard to think if I could've gotten back to Wabash from Terre Haute, having been moved spiritually by my grandparents, and went about trying to re-create the scene for myself on a sow. I don't think I did, I'll tell myself, but there's always that doubt. Somewhere, down deep inside, I do remember losing my hunger and finding it again, and it's that memory, so firm and completely distinct, that makes me think I am the original, unimitated, wholly found Pig Boy. It's as close to a confession as I can muster, at least for now.

When Grandfathers Steal Pigs

2

My grandfather snuck onto my farm without my knowing it. It was 1975 and we'd just moved to our fifth cash-rented farm, meaning that for the most part we were sharecroppers, raising hogs and growing mostly corn to feed them. Any grain left over went to Mr. Grady, the man who owned the place. When we moved, I concluded that the new farm was somehow mine. I told people as much when my dad would ask me whose place we were farming. Embarrassed, I would shrug my shoulders and say quietly, "Mine." He'd chuckle. "What was that?" he'd say, holding his hand to his ear. I'd say again, "Mine." And whoever was standing with my dad at the grain elevator would rub my head and tell me, "That's the way to go, boy!"

I was hurt when I found out that the farm wasn't really ours, much less mine. I was too young to remember any of the other places we'd rented, and when we moved to the Grady farm I thought all the talking my parents had done about getting their own farm had finally come true. I felt sorry for them. I made it worse by thinking they'd gotten it when they in fact hadn't. I remember wrapping up my plastic barnyard set, the same kind you can still buy now for children, and giving it to my father for his birthday. When he opened it, he seemed more embarrassed than I was. Later, he put it back with my other things in the bedroom I shared with Derrick and Darren. It looked ugly to me, and I can't recall ever playing with it again.

That spring I was seven and had found a sow and her fifteen baby pigs in our barn. I'd been playing in the haymow alone. The rest of the kids were inside the house watching cartoons, a rare experience since we usually had to work most of the time on Saturday mornings, when *Scooby-Doo* and the others aired. But I liked being outside, exploring on my own, and this morning I was above the manger, trying to build a straw bale fort like the ones I'd seen Derrick and Darren expertly put together.

I tugged on a moldy bale; pigeons exploded from the dark hand-hewn rafters; a ray of sun piped through a knothole near the high roof and shone into my eyes, making me squint hard. I heard something downstairs below my feet, where we usually kept only sacks of feed and spare tractor parts. I wobbled to the steep ladder and crawled down the brittle rungs. I was a very plump child, usually full of the only thing I would consent to eat: mashed potatoes. I flopped off the end of the ladder and waddled to the hallway behind the manger and peeked through an old milking stall into the dusty granary. A bulky sow lay on her side, slimy little creatures struggling about her belly, wobbling and bobbing from one erect nipple to the other, trying to get their first sip of earthly food.

I crouched down in my bib overalls and watched. Something that sounded like suction came from the sow's rear. I crawled on my hands and knees in the dirt and hard cow pies left by the livestock of the cash renter before us. When I'd finished creeping into the L of the manger, I was directly behind the sow, just a couple of feet from her tail. I'd not seen anything born yet, and as I looked upon the sow's bloody backside, a thick strand of afterbirth jiggling and pulsating as she breathed and pushed and groaned, I felt I was doing something wrong, perhaps witnessing a kind of violence. I watched as a little black-and-white chunk flopped out of the sow's butt, the place I thought any baby thing came from. The piglet lay on its side, not moving, and a sniffle started in my runny nose. I thought the very first thing I'd seen born had died. I assumed that by watching it I'd caused the death. Tears blurred my vision, and I wiped my eyes with a hanky from my overalls pouch. I'd started carrying one of the white-and-red kerchiefs with me because it made me look like a real live, grown-up hog man, something I wanted desperately to be. A hog man, not a pig boy.

As I tucked the wet hanky back into my front pouch, the sow grunted while the newborns suckled the smooth, white expanse of her underbelly. I tried to count the babies but couldn't. The little black-and-white pig still wasn't moving. I felt a sting in my throat. All at once, after the sow made a noise that sounded like a bark, another pig shot out of her with such force that it knocked into the one I'd killed with my eyes. Quickly, I looked away, fearful that if I watched the new one, it too would find its fate at the receiving end of my stare.

I kept my head turned for several minutes and remained on all fours in the manger. I decided that if I could steal a quick look through my fingers, the piglets would be OK; a quick glance would surely leave them intact. I opened a slat between two fingers and peered out. I could smell the dry manure on my palms from crawling. My eyes got accustomed to the light and I could see the two pigs. Now a blob of blood and veins hung out of the sow, and a large clear sac bubbled forth as well. I focused and could see both of the last-born pigs squirming to get on their feet; they pulled hard at their umbilical cords like miniature Budweiser horses at a sleigh. I took my hand from my face, sure now that all was fine. The other newborn piglet was a dark red, and I grew happier watching how the two babies tried to outdo each other. Finally the black-and-white piglet broke free; its cord snapped and flew back with force into its mother's mess. In a few more pulls the red piglet broke free too, and I was wide-eyed at how the two of them knew where to go for food. They stumbled and fell as they joined their siblings at the full row of rosy teats, tiny wet heads bobbing and poking as they filled their stomachs with warm milk.

I wanted badly to hold the piglets, but I knew from hearing the men talk that a mother sow could be very protective of her young. Once, while I was sitting at the kitchen table with my father and grandfather drinking coffee and eating pancakes and sausage, my dad told a story about a man he knew in another county. The man had been trying to wean a litter of pigs from their mother. The sow was away for a few moments, scrounging the pasture for weeds and nuts, when he decided to use a burlap bag to gather up the piglets. He jumped the fence and began catching the lightning-fast pigs, stuffing them squealing into the bag to carry them into the next barn, where they'd be given a nice pen with an automatic corn feeder. He was about done when he heard something at the entrance to the shed. The sow was on him before he could even turn to try and jump the fence. She torn off a large section of his bicep and did the same to his calf before he finally managed to get a leg up and over the fence. When my father was finished telling the story, my grandfather said, "Damn fool. Everyone knows you got to thump a pig once between the eyes before you put them in the bag. Numbs them for a while. Keeps them quiet."

I stood up in the manger aisle and brushed off my overalls. I'd decided the best thing to do was go tell my father about the sow and piglets, then bother him until he let me help with the babies. There were vitamins to give them with a syringe into their soft mouths, and a quick shot of antibiotics for them and their mother too, just under the skin behind the left ear. It'd hurt, and they'd squeal in protest, but the shot fought off the scours, a deadly intestinal sickness that could leave an entire litter dead in just a few hours if not treated, or dehydrated and weak, ochre diarrhea over them all if they did manage to live.

I tiptoed through the barn to the front door. Just as I was about to pull the door open to the bright outside, I paused to look out through a crack in the door. I saw my grandfather coming toward the barn on a muddy tractor. I snuck back into the spot where I'd been, the sow now raising her head from time to time to sniff the occasional piglet that wandered from nipple to snout. It looked like she was kissing them. The little pigs would scurry back to the others when their mother touched them with her cold, wet nose. The scene made me laugh, but I put my hand over my mouth and crouched back down to hide from my grandfather.

He walked quickly into the barn. Light flooded over the old feeding stalls, making them look more like chrome than wood. I tucked myself deeper into my corner, where cobwebs filled the space between two beams, thick like cotton candy. My grandfather walked right up to the partition, moved a pitchfork, leaned it on a board behind him, and looked over the plank at the sow. I was angry that he knew about her. Back then I assumed he knew everything, especially those things that made me happy, and was always there to draw the line between what was supposed to be serious farm work and what could be fun. All the pregnant sows, once they were close to full term (three months, three weeks, and three days of gestation), went to his farm across the pasture to the farrowing house. He treated the building with a no-nonsense regimen that did not allow us kids to pet or hold the baby pigs. We were to clean underneath the stalls and feed the sows but were not to touch the baby pigs, creating in me a feeling that he was a cruel man, a man who didn't know how good he had it.

I tried to make my body collapse into the small space, but my bottom was full figured and I could only manage to inch back slightly. I wore Derrick and Darren's hand-me-down overalls; they were made for stocky boys, and, for me, my mother had to hem them so much that the seam made a band just an inch or so below my fleshy knees. I sucked in my belly and tried to breathe silently, allowing only a snippet of air out, exhaling through my nose in precise intervals, which I believed would keep me from drawing my grandfather's attention to the corner.

He had always been skinny, and, with the light behind him, he appeared to be frozen on a pole for a moment, a scarecrow waiting for something to happen. He watched the sow like that for what seemed to be half a day, then left the barn, the door still open, clearly a sign he was coming back. He strode back through the door carrying a gunnysack in his hand. When he picked out a spot that was best to climb into the pen with the sow, he nearly stepped on the end of my work boot. I held my breath completely. Once into the pen, he slowly walked to the back end of the sow. He examined the afterbirth and the pigs. I thought I saw him holding his breath, too. The sow didn't notice him; she was grunting rhythmically, easing into a nap, as the piglets nursed less eagerly, some of them falling asleep as well.

Grandfather squatted down by the sow and with a quick dash of his thin hand nabbed a spotted pig off a nipple. He turned the piglet around in his hand and thumped the little thing right between the eyes, tossing it into the sack so quickly he looked like a magician putting on a show. I stepped out from where I'd been hiding, unsure of what to do. I felt anger at the old man. Heat swelled in my round shoulders. I could feel real hate pulling me out further from the dark corner. My feet made a scuffing sound in the loose cement and pieces of stray grain. The old man picked up a pig that was entirely white. He thumped it and pushed it into the bag. I swayed from side to side with pent-up energy, wanting to stop him but not knowing how. He caught a glimpse of me in the corner of his eye. He turned his head slowly and looked at me with an intense stare. He was caught himself. If he said something, the sow would know he was there. She might wake up and take a hunk out of him, but if he didn't quiet me down, he could expect the same outcome. I knew he wanted to whip me good right then, but he simply put a finger to his lips and winked at me. I knew that later he'd have a talk with my father about how careless I'd been. It wouldn't make a difference what I did, I decided.

I turned to walk away slowly and my grandfather must've thought he'd scared me enough that I was going to the house, and I was, but then, as he snapped up another baby pig when my back was to him, and I heard the thump of his mean finger against the soft skull of another piglet, I passed the pitchfork and latched onto it and rushed back to the partition. My grandfather looked ready to risk the bite of the sow on his thin leg to lay into me good with a switch. His eyes turned whiter around the edges when I tried to yell at him. I was sobbing now, and the pitchfork shook as I pointed it at him over the gate. The thickness in my throat made me feel weak, like I'd never be a man, ever; no matter how hard I tried, I would remain a chubby little snotnose incapable of doing what a man had to do.

"Put my pigs down," I sputtered, the rough handle of my weapon bouncing; I turned the prongs upward as my grandfather stepped toward me. In a second he was out of the pen, near the front door of the barn before I could say anything else. He held in his hand the sack with several of the baby pigs in it; they started to make faint squeaks. The sow stirred at the commotion, began to snort and huff. I was scared that she would leap the stall and tear into me, thinking I'd stolen some of her babies. My grandfather stomped around for a couple of seconds. He turned inside the frame of the bright doorway and spoke. I couldn't see anything but his outline, dark and tall, stiff as the beams of the barn. "Son, get your little ass over here. That sow's all worked up now. She's likely to come at you right through that gate."

I didn't want to go to him, but I was terrified that the sow, now on her feet sniffing the afterbirth and turning circles, looking for vanished babies, was going to get me. I let the pitchfork fall. It rattled, and the sow started to pant and growl. I could see my grandfather hesitate, then take a step away from the doorway. When he got to me he took me by the shoulder, tight; his fingers dug into my skin. It hurt and was meant to. He said in a low, angry voice, a kind of hiss that can only be made through clenched teeth, "You'll never get to be a hog man acting like that."

Later, he would tell my dad how I had gotten in the way and that he should sit me down and explain some things. From that time on, my grandfather teased me and called me Pig Boy. It was meant to be half joke and half insult, an ongoing comment on how I needed to toughen up.

I shot out the barn door to the silver light of the paddock. It was late morning; the sun was warm on my face, and as I ran I could feel the tears drying. I'd stay in the rows of the cornfield until my mother called me to the house. In the dirt I dug a hole with my hands, hoping I could escape to whatever better place was below this farm that wasn't ours.

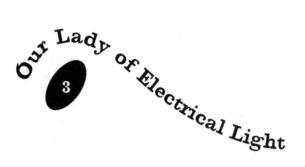

Our Lady of Electrical Light

3

The Grady farm sat just outside the city limits of Wabash, Indiana, where a sign read: The First Electrically Lighted City in the World.

Charles Brush, the inventor of the first carbon-arc lightbulb, lit up the banks of the Wabash River with so much artificial light that the last remaining tribes of Miami Indians watched in total dismay as the white man's town bore a sun from its middle. The crude electrical switch was thrown in March 1880, one of the darkest nights of the year.

It has been said that when our forebearers were first introduced to electric lights, they tended to stare right at them, and then report with disdain that the lights had caused them not to be able to see *anything at all.* Fliers were printed and handed out that told the citizens not to stare directly at the lights. Much of where I am from is still like that; we have a tendency in the Midwest to look directly at something for quite some time before we are able to find the right words to articulate exactly what it is we're seeing. That's not being dull-witted, by any means. We like to think of it as being purposeful and reflective.

It has also been reported that it took people several months to stop staring at the lights at night, even after several town hall speeches insisted that people stop looking directly into the lights; some signs were even posted, but still the phenomenon persisted. If you ever drive through Wabash, at night, of course, don't be surprised if there's some middle-aged man standing on the corner of Pike Street and Wabash Avenue, dumbfounded, head tilted toward the sky, gawking at the marvel of electricity. I'm proud of that; after all, it's been over 120 years since the town made history with light and we're still in awe; that's a life philosophy at work, not stupidity. We can all see that.

From the end of the lane, which was bordered on one side by the hog pasture and on the other with a field of corn, we could shoot a BB gun and hit the green sign that told drivers on Pike Street they were about to leave the country and enter the town. The only differences between the two were an ordinance that stated a person couldn't keep livestock inside the city limits, and the fact that once you passed the farm, the houses on the remainder of Pike Street were closer together. People still kept chickens and some sheep behind their houses, but for the most part the Grady farm was the beacon that relayed to travelers that what lay before them was an endless stretch of agricultural bliss, one that rolled on for miles until the limestone bluffs redirected them toward the swanky metropolises of Marion, Fort Wayne, and Kokomo, where all was lost, and the world became nothing but crime and decadence.

Shortly after the incident with the baby pigs, I stopped talking to anyone in my family. They didn't seem to notice. Several times I took my red Kool-Aid canteen I'd sent off for and went on a walkabout in the pasture, telling myself that if I could tame one of the massive crossbred boars into letting me ride him, I'd be on my way into the city of Wabash. I dreamed about getting an apartment near the river, forgetting everything I could about becoming a hog man, and getting a job working at the Burger's Dairy store just up the street from where the bridge crossed the river. Our school bus drove over it every day going and coming from Southwood Elementary. I'd peer out the window at the muddy river below, thinking about all the stories we'd been told about Wabash and light. The *Fort Wayne Gazette* called it "the strangest light ever exhibited in the United States."

Every year, the grade school classes went on a field trip to look at the first real lightbulb. It was kept under glass in the court-house. On a Friday in late spring we once again were bussed in to take a gander.

I got off the bus with the rest of my class and searched the lines of kids traipsing into the courthouse for Darren, the one person I wanted most to be like. I'd already given up on not talking to him, and I wanted badly to walk into the courthouse with him and his friends, who were four grades ahead of me. I was in the habit of carrying a workingman's lunch box, replete with silver thermos, which I filled with coffee. All my classmates carried boxes with *Welcome Back, Kotter* scenes or the Fonz on them, but I pre-ferred to go to school with my drab olive lunchbox with a plas-tic black handle and shiny rivets showing on the ends and back.

I spotted my brother Darren way up in front of the line, stand-ing on the steps of the courthouse, a flock of his friends around him, all with flannel shirts on, thermal underwear underneath, rolled up on their forearms, the flannel and off-white thermal material in a bunch at their elbows. They looked as tough and cool as anything I could've imagined. I felt like a stocky dwarf with absolutely no flair for farm dress. I looked down at my own shirt, a white Texas number with plastic pearl snap buttons, fading poinsettias embroidered over the pockets, a homemade jobby from my mother. I'd loved the shirt up to that moment, but right then, watching Darren entering the courthouse, I wanted to strip it off and hide it under the bus, wedge it up between the tailpipe and the steel bus floor, and run down the street to the co-op to steal a real man's shirt. I untucked the shirt from my pants and stayed in line behind a kid from inside the city limits who liked to punch me as hard as he could in the shoulder and make farting noises when I walked down the hall so the girls in front of me would turn around, giggling, thinking I'd done the dirty deed. I remained quiet so he wouldn't notice I was behind him. I looked over the crowd again and could no longer see Darren anywhere. You didn't have to go to school on field trip day, and Dina and Dana had remained home to help my mother with canning. Derrick was in high school, taking Vo-Ag classes, and was part of a class building a house for credit.

As we filed past the lightbulb in the glass case, each student was supposed to stand and look at it for the time it took to count to five in your head. But the kids had made a joke out of the process; I could hear the older kids counting very loudly. The teachers and volunteer parents tried to redirect them, saying, "Come on, now, let's have some respect here. Electricity is part of Wabash's history. It's part of your history, too." But the kids kept on counting out loud anyway.

I was getting close to the front of the line; about ten kids stood before me. I caught a glimpse of Darren filing out the door back to the buses. He stood in line again, waiting for the exit. There was a ray of sun slanting into the building through the oval windows at the peak of the balcony surrounding the interior of the courthouse. The light shone down on Darren and his friends. I watched him with envy. He was tall and thin, having outgrown his pudge, while I was still layered with baby fat, rutilant cheeks glowing like apples. He had his thumbs thrust into the loops of a wide leather belt; his hands hung down, strong, the tips of his fingers touching the front of his jeans. I admired how manly his wrists looked as he shrugged his shoulders at a question one of his friends had asked. He was the opposite of me in every way, I thought. Our grandfather often commented on how hard a worker he was, how he had a good head for farming. Darren learned to weld early and was called on by my grandfather to mend the metal crates in the farrowing house, where I assumed they shared secrets and got to play with the baby pigs all they wanted.

I kept on watching him as my line approached the lightbulb case and his line grew closer to the exit. I began to hear snickers, which bubbled up into a steadier round of laughter. The sound of a faraway voice made me let loose of my gaze on my brother. A teacher named Mrs. Norman was speaking curtly in my direction.

"Douglas. Douglas," she said, louder, irritated with my daydreaming. I turned to see that I was holding up the line. I'd gotten so lost in watching Darren that the last kid to take his viewing of the almighty bulb was now over in the line with him. I had my hands tucked into my belt like my brother and had moved slightly to the right of the line. My face grew red hot as I walked briskly to the glass case. For a moment, I couldn't think of what I was supposed to do there. My mind was still full of other visions, of me as a successful hog farmer, my arms and legs and hands capable in every way to perform what was needed to be manly and competent, thin and muscular. I stood in front of the case and looked dumbly at the bulb. It was made of smoky blue glass, the filament inside like the hookworms our grandfather talked about, telling us how if we ever saw such a worm to take action, call the vet and scrub down everything in sight with bleach. Hog cholera, he'd said, was worse than the devil. It could leave pig and sow alike with no more than a pint of blood left in their whole body. If the blood flukes got to our hogs, we'd better hope we died, too.

Standing there, my stubby arms at my side, I decided the thing under the glass case was a warning, a sign, one that I was certain would lead my parents to their dreams. Mrs. Norman sounded angry with me. "Douglas! Move on now. For goodness' sake, you're to count to five and go!" She shooed me away, holding her hands like she was showing off a new manicure, or pretending to hop like an upright bunny. Before I took a step, a boy near Darren yelled, "Move it, Pig Boy!" The inside of the courthouse echoed with a burst of laughter. I didn't look up as I stepped across the front of the case and got into the back of the line for the exit. When I was able to manage looking up, I could no longer see Darren, but I imagined his hands and how they could weld and dock the tails of pigs and perform all the things a man could do, my grandfather inspecting his deft movements with something like a gleam in his eye.

Chores and Sex Ed

4

The next day, Saturday, my mother sat at the kitchen table with a spiral notebook before her. She was punching a tablet-sized calculator and scrawling down numbers on the lined sheets of paper, two columns in neat printing, pressed hard enough to show into the next page, like always. When I'd use her paper to draw a picture or write a story, I'd run my fingers over the blank sheet, the Braille of her and my father's dreams. I would strain to try and make out the digits, hoping I could find a figure that meant they were going to make it. But all I could ever decipher were the 8s and 2s, nothing else, and so I decided their inability to achieve their goal had to do with the even numbers.

All the other kids (Darren, Derrick, Dina, and Dana) were sitting around the table, eating Wheaties, the one cereal my mother, Doris, and our dad, Dan, would allow us to buy from the store. The clerks there called us the 7 D's, which my mother loved and used to sign the Christmas cards she sent out each year. Darren had the sugar can next to his bowl, scooping out generous amounts and spooning more and more onto a heap that was already covering the entire top of his cereal. Dina and Dana wore Precious Moments nightgowns that my mother had made herself. Darren was already dressed while Derrick wore the same print pajamas as all us boys. They had a blue background with yellow smiley faces all in bright abundance.

My mother looked up from her math. "Sit down, Dougie, and eat." She had scotch tape on her bangs; the strips pulled at the skin above her eyebrows, crinkling it, making her look upset. I wasn't very hungry but fixed myself a bowl anyway. Darren pulled a chair out for me to sit down. I wasn't mad at him about the day before at the courthouse; I knew he hadn't had anything to do with the kid calling me Pig Boy. The nickname had stuck; by the time I entered school and insisted on my mother helping me to bring baby pigs for show-and-tell, it was cemented. We went to a grade school that was going through an integration of sorts. As more and more subdivisions were built inside the city limits to accommodate the white-collar jobs that the General Tire and Ford Meter Box factories created, the more our classes filled with kids who'd never been on a farm. The kids from inside the city limits were amazed at the baby pigs I brought to class in cardboard boxes. Their questions about what the pigs ate and how their tails got stubby filled me with great pride. While I was shy, I loved to talk about how the baby pigs were born with their eyes open, how they took vitamins just like kids, and how they'd grow to weigh over two hundred pounds. When they saw me in the hall or on the playground they'd yell "Pig Boy!" and point at me.

Darren spoke with a mouth full of sugar and Wheaties. "Dad's taking Grandma and Grandpa to Terre Haute today. We have to do all the chores. He's already gone."

I looked at my mom, who was still busy tallying up what they had in the bank from selling some corn from the drying bin. Feeling me look at her, she spoke. "It's true. You boys are to feed the sows and turn the boars in with the new group of gilts. Your dad will be back tomorrow morning." She didn't look up as she punched the keys on the calculator, the empty cog where a roll of ticker tape should go clicking like mad.

It was exciting news. My grandfather had been having some health problems and had been told by his doctor to take a break from the farm for a couple weeks. He was not happy about it, but my father had been able to convince him to rest by using the trip as an excuse. Grandpa's other son, Courtney, still lived around Terre Haute and had recently purchased a team of draft horses. My dad had told his father, "He needs you to take a look at them. He said he wants your opinion on how to train them."

While my mother tapped out her figures, Darren talked about what we needed to do for the day. Although Derrick was the oldest, he let Darren come up with how we would go about the chores. The girls and my mom were going to the grocery store and over to the fabric store to begin picking out material for the dresses they were making for the 4-H fair in August.

With the last of his cereal still in his mouth, Darren got up and went to the sink to rinse his bowl. He was in the habit of talking so fast that only those right next to him could make any sense out of it. He said with a clipped surge, "We better get out there now and get going. Let's turn the boars out first. You know it will take a while to get them corralled and over into the other pasture. After that we can feed the old sows and start on the feed sacks from there."

Derrick has always had big, droopy eyes, the kind a basset hound has, long eyelashes thick and black, and now he looked tired just listening to Darren rattle on about our chores. Still, I was excited to get to really help out with the hogs without my grandfather or dad around, hoping that I'd be able to secretly siphon off some of my older brothers' know-how and be ready to show off my new skills when my father returned from Terre Haute.

Our mother told us to be careful as she and the girls backed out of the lane in the rickety old station wagon. She told Darren, "Watch Dougie that he don't get hurt." I didn't like her saying that and waited until the car was out of the lane before I said anything.

"That bitch doesn't know what she's talking about," I said. Derrick and Darren looked like two Mr. Bills standing in the gravel. I wanted to take it back before it even left my mouth, but I thought it was a good way to sound tough and older. Derrick and Darren laughed as they tugged me by the arms toward the barns, one on each side of me. "Dougie," Darren said, "you better start acting right or Pig Boy is going to get sent to market." We all laughed then as we strode in our gum boots out over the flat land to the pigs, our boots, too big on all of our feet, flopping wildly, the combined sound like a flat tire going over pavement. Our dog, Joe, trailed along after us. He was a gift from our maternal grandparents, who we rarely saw. They sent my mother some money and, because we'd heard about a Saturday morning show, which wasn't a cartoon, called *Run, Joe, Run,* about a German shepherd performing brave and noble rescues, we named him after the show. It disappeared from TV after one season.

Once when Joe was a puppy we convinced our parents to let all five Ds watch the show, postponing our chores for an hour or so. We put the puppy on the floor in front of the TV and circled him, lying down with pillows to watch. The production quality was bad, and it was easy to tell that the producers had used several different German shepherds in the taping. In one scene Joe would be nearly all black, just a trace of autumn around his paws, and in the next it was as if the Joe from before had been fitted for a taupe vest that encased her middle section. From scene to scene the Joe changed and grew, sometimes thinner, often with less fullness in its coat, and a few action shots clearly showed a mixed breed performing the stunts. When it was over, Dina rubbed our Joe on his head. "Don't worry," she said. "We won't let them do that to you."

After that we had no desire to watch the program again. I've often wondered if viewing the program imprinted Joe. Did he figure that he would have to change to survive on the farm? Was he aware of the many forms he could take? He would go through his own mutations and suffer dearly for it, along with the many other creatures he essentially tortured, but initially he was a great companion and seemed suitable for life on a farm.

As we neared the pen where we kept our boars, Joe shot past us after a groundhog that had holed up under an old planter. I called after Joe but he was jumping the fence by then, his tail curled in a stiff loop as he disappeared into the verdant cornfield.

The boars we had were always mixed-breed sell-offs from our neighbors' hog operations. We couldn't afford to buy young, purebred stock, so we ended up with middle-aged has-beens with coarse hair and swollen balls. The two boars were lying on their sides near the barn, shit caked to their butts and their ample nuts wrinkly and bald. I'd never gotten this close to them before, and as we approached Darren told us to wait until he got the gate open to the new pasture to rile them from their sleep. He jogged away from us and unlatched the gate to the green grass; it swung on its hinges, squeaking all the way until it hit the stone stopper. Darren now ran back at us, his hands poised to work.

"OK," he said. "Let's get them up." Darren motioned for me to stand back as he and Derrick used wooden canes to gently nudge the boars' ears, pulling them upward so that the morning sunshine would wake them. The boars grunted and began to stand, dust escaping from their enormous hides in swirls of gray. They stank. The aroma of manure and something pungent wafted up into our faces. Our grandfather called that smell *gamy;* he said that it was the stink that got the females ready to mate. I wondered if he smelled that way for my grandmother Rose, or if my dad tried to get that funky for my mother. It was all too scary to think about.

We were not a fancy operation. Our sows were free range, and when they came into estrus we simply put the boars in with them for several weeks, until we'd look out and see the old coots dozing by a fence, their work completed, ready to be pulled back into confinement with one another, eating all the crushed corn and watermelon rinds their saggy guts could bear.

Darren drove the boars slowly to the entrance to the pasture. As they walked they grunted, sniffing the air, trying to get a reading on what was waiting for them. The gilts waiting in the pasture were an assortment of colors, from entirely solid russet to black and white to belted markings and oval spots. Some even had each leg a different color. We had mixed the breeds of Duroc, Hampshire, and Landrace over and over so many times that when the litters were born the crates filled with every imaginable combination, a Benetton commercial for the porky set.

Derrick and I sat on the fence while Darren pushed the gate shut. I had the same body type as my oldest brother, Derrick, compact and stocky, while Darren was lean and taut. I watched Darren now. His arms flexed while he wrapped wire around the gate to keep it in place. The boars lifted their heads, turning up their snouts, sucking in the scent of the gilts huddled in a mass under a large oak tree. The gilts looked spooked. They were less than a year old, and roughly two hundred pounds each, but the boars were four times that size, and ancient.

Darren climbed onto the fence with us. I hooked my boots the way he did on the white rungs. I felt like a hog man. I was going to make it as a farmer, I thought, as we watched the boars rumble toward the herd. Most of the gilts darted toward the back of the pasture, but a few of them stayed still, nervous but in heat, incapable of doing anything but waiting for nature to take its course. I'd not been privy to much of anything yet in terms of mating, and as I watched, wide-eyed, Darren decided it was time to move on to the other chores. He jumped down from the fence. So did Derrick. The boars sniffed under the tails of two white gilts. "Come on down from there, Dougie." Darren smiled at Derrick. "We've got to feed those sows now."

I wouldn't budge. I knew nothing about sex, or about how anything was created on the earth, and I didn't want to take my eyes off what I thought was going to be informational. My friend Mark, who lived on a modern farm with lots of new buildings and shiny tractors, told me that pigs and other animals had to do what a man does inside a woman if there's going to be babies. He'd whispered to me at recess, "The man thing has to pee inside the woman's hole to make babies." I was amazed and confounded. When I peed it was nothing spectacular, certainly not anything I thought a woman would find appealing. I assumed that was the gaminess my grandfather talked about. After all, sometimes my pee did smell when I let it splash on the barn siding.

Darren approached me at the fence, took off his Funk's Seed Corn hat by the bill, and swatted at my stubby legs. "Come on," he insisted. "Get down from there, Dougie. I'll let you turn the auger on when we do the feeding." I wasn't about to be enticed from the fence. One of the boars had mounted a gilt. Her legs trembled from his weight as brown froth from his whiskery snout dropped onto her back and ran down her sides like shook-up cola. I watched intently as something long and pink spiraled out from the other boar's belly, who stood by his cohort, sniffing everything that oinked. It looked like a giant corkscrew. Years later, I'd read how the colloquialism "to screw" was derived from the shape of the porcine penis. I thought my wee-wee was going to grow into what I saw flailing in the grass, no less than a yard long and coated in slime, the likes of which I'd only seen in a horror movie. It was terrifying to ponder.

Derrick climbed back onto the fence and tried to cover my eyes with his hand. I brushed it aside. We were all about four years apart; Derrick was sixteen, Darren twelve, and I'd just turned eight. They knew things I didn't, and they wanted to keep me from watching. Derrick tried again to put his hand over my peepers, but I scooted further away on the fence.

"You might as well let him see now," Darren said. "He's already got the main idea of it anyway." Derrick leaped from the fence into the grass. His hat fell off, and Darren picked it up and handed it to him. They walked to the fence, laughing, and stood with their backs against the white planks, waiting for me to get an eyeful and get on with the chores. Both boars were now in hunching mode, the poor creatures under them about to capsize. It looked ridiculous, something I told myself I'd never want to play a part in with a human lady.

"I hope that one doesn't fall asleep again," Darren snorted. Talking directly to Derrick, he said, "Remember last year when he fell off that old crippled sow and didn't wake up even when he hit the ground?" They laughed so hard that the sound spooked the virgin gilts hiding at the back of the pasture; the herd rumbled toward the lean-to, cramming into it like a phone booth prank.

And that was that. The boars had been at the mating game so long that they had learned to climax together. They dismounted at the same time, leaving the deflowered females wobbly-legged and weak, shuddering as they retreated toward the others in the shed. The boars lay down right where they had just bred, rolled some in the slimy grass to cover their bodies in pheromones, and were out like lights in seconds.

I sat on the fence feeling disgusted. I didn't like that the gross, sloppy boars had hurt the gilts. I jumped down and found a stone. Before either of my brothers could stop me, I hurled it toward the boars. It fell short, of course, landing just a few feet in front of me. Darren walked up behind me and took me by the shoulders. "Come on," he said. "We better get to work." He sounded sad, as if he'd let me down by allowing me to witness such a thing at my age. The three of us walked out of the pasture together toward the barn lot. I felt like crying, but held it in. Darren noticed the forced hyperinhales I was making to keep from losing it. He nudged Derrick in the ribs and grabbed me by the arm. We stood still for a moment. Darren said, already kneeling down in a racing position, "On your mark..." I smiled and bent down. I regained my breathing as I tried to imitate him. They were in the habit of letting me win in footraces, which meant they had to nearly walk so that my chubby arms could paddle the air and get out ahead of them. Derrick played along and readied himself at the starting line. "Get set. Go!" My brothers seemed to lose their lead instantly. Behind us, the boars snored loudly. It sounded like our father. I passed Derrick first, then Darren, and ended up in the barn lot way before they stopped cheering me on.

Wicked Birds
5

The Saturday my fingers were mauled I distinctly recall seeing blackbirds everywhere. They clung to the electrical wires that draped from several small outbuildings to the large red barn in the center of the farm. The birds called from the walnut trees and hopped among the combed-over swatches of fescue in the steaming pasture. Some swooped down through the cool air to peck at the corn spilled before the tires of our John Deere. Our dog Joe, who was generally less than helpful around the farm, chased the birds around the barn lot. Twice before the morning of the accident, other farmers had shot at Joe after they'd allegedly caught him chasing their pigs. There were blackbirds everywhere I looked. The entire paddock was filled with them. Rows upon rows of the birds roosted on the wires; they chattered along the peaks of the aluminum roofs and pecked along the ground near the corncrib. I watched as the blackbirds swooped down from their perches to wrestle with another in the dirt, fluttering, cawing, and preening. Derrick and

Darren were in the old milk house where we kept the five-gallon buckets used for hauling the corn from the auger to the sows in the front pasture. It was grueling work. We had to carry one bucket for every two sows, which meant that by the time we were done we would've lifted twenty of the heavy buckets over the fence. I waited for my brothers to come back, the birds swarming over the farm in waves of black, the sky twisting and turning, forever shifting as the flocks scoured the bright blue sky.

When Derrick and Darren came toward me, balancing a high stack of empty buckets as if they were performing some tandem trick for the circus, I began to pester them.

"You said I could turn the auger on. You said." I loved flipping the toggle switch near the belt and drive, where the corn would magically spill out in sudden spurts, the coiling steel of the auger grinding and shaking the hefty motor welded to the side of the bin.

"OK," said Darren. "But I don't want you telling Mom and Dad we didn't watch you good." He spit onto the ground as we walked in the direction of the corncrib. I tagged after them, as they peered around the wobbling buckets to see where they were stepping, the handles clapping against the metal in rhythm.

"If you don't let me turn it on . . ." I paused, unsure if I should now downgrade my respectable hog man status by acting the brat, but I really loved to turn on the switch. "I'll tell them you let me watch the pigs doing it."

"OK," Darren said, irritated that I'd resorted to such a threat when he was going to hold up his end of the bargain anyway.

The crib held over twenty thousand bushels of shelled corn. Grady, our landlord, had built it after he'd heard he might be able to make more money on the grain if we kept it stored until the market wasn't so saturated in the spring. It was an expensive structure, normally reserved for farm owners who had worked long enough to pay down their debt and therefore had the luxury of splurging on such a wise addition to the farm. But Grady had plenty of money and he wanted more; it was one of many ideas he'd wanted to talk to my dad about after reading an article from *Prairie Farmer* in his swank apartment inside the city limits.

I stood back, away from the auger, and flipped the switch when Darren nodded his OK. Derrick handed Darren an empty bucket after the one he held under the auger filled with dry, orange, shelled corn. The corn pinged off the bottom of the metal bucket as it rushed in. Darren would struggle to pass the full bucket to Derrick and quickly push another empty one under the flowing corn. The auger had an exposed belt drive. Two metal pulleys, one as big as a dinner plate and the other the circumference of a saucer, turned the tight belt that made the long metal auger, hidden deep inside the metal bin, gather corn from the center of the mound inside and bring it out to our buckets. Sometimes the corn from the middle of the bin was wet, and it slowed the auger down, making it stall, then slightly lurch, and finally break the wet clod free enough to return to normal.

Darren had Derrick step forward with an empty bucket as he hurried to move out of the way, then motioned to me to turn off the auger. It made a stalling sound right when I shut it off, like it had already stopped before I did anything. All ten buckets were filled, and it was time to lug them to the pasture. Darren picked up a heavy bucket in each hand. So did Derrick.

"Don't move from there, OK?" Darren commanded. "And don't mess around with the switch." They were off then, toting the corn to the sows, their backs hunched over. A large swarm of blackbirds immediately fell from the sky onto the loose corn under the auger's mouth. They pecked and screeched, jumping on top of each other, fighting for the best position. I thought of the boar's wicked tool from earlier, how much the shape of it resembled an auger; they were both corkscrews. The blackbirds picked the ground clean in a matter of seconds and burst back up from the ground to rest on the sows' backs at the feeding troughs.

It was quiet once the birds flapped off, and I could hear the buckets of corn spilling into metal; it reminded me of my mason jar of change when I dumped it on my bed to count it. Something hummed inside the bin. It churned and vibrated; clearly something was stuck. I pressed my ear against the metal and tried to listen, my hand still tight around the toggle switch. I did what I was told not to. I flipped the switch. No corn came out of the auger, but the hum inside eased. I flicked the switch off and on quickly. Each time the noise went from a purr to a whine and back again. I was amazed at how my action would cause the change. I smelled something, corn and rubber burning, like the midway at the fairgrounds. I flipped the switch double-time. The auger now moved some, and a few spurts of shelled corn like buckshot fell to the ground. I looked to see if my brothers were coming; they weren't. I moved away from my station against the bin.

The auger smelled hot; the oil and sulfur made me pinch my nose. I tapped the metal to see if it was warm. I pulled my hand back and sniffed my fingers. The drone inside the bin got louder. I looked over my shoulder and saw only the empty lot. I wanted to touch the rubber belt. I'd seen Darren try and turn it by hand when the corn inside was too wet to risk burning up the motor. I decided that was what was making the hum inside the bin; the auger was stuck in mushy corn. I could fix it. I reached for the belt with my right hand and wrapped my fingers around it. The rubber was taut and warm. I wanted to show my brothers that I could do more than pester them. I thought if I could turn the belt by hand they'd come back with their empty buckets and slap me on the back and tell me how great a farmer I was going to make.

A few stray sows milled around the bin. They were older stock, left alone to heal from torn teats or hoof infections. I watched them nibble a few stalks of volunteer corn that had sprouted up near a concrete slab. They looked up at me, their snouts twitching, taking in my scent. I talked to them. "Hey there, mamas." I made a soft pig call I'd heard other farmers use. It was made by forming your lips as if about to kiss, popping top lip on bottom in rapid but gentle succession. It was meant to sound like water dripping in a sink. The sows grunted and went on eating. I smiled at how they could understand me and turned my attention back to the belt drive.

I pulled on the belt, but nothing happened. The sound didn't change like it had before with the switch. I yanked on the belt again, and it lurched. Something hot and terrible shot up my right arm, an ugly, repetitive vibration that tossed me to the ground. The last thing I saw was the sick sows moving toward me as I lay on my side on the soft ground, their wet noses crinkled in worry, like how they looked when one of their babies was stuck in a fence. I closed my eyes as the motor and auger, running freely, buried my feet in a mound of corn.

I woke faceup in the tractor's scoop loader when Darren came rushing back out of the house. I could see the blackbirds overhead calling and calling and I thought they were the buzzards from the Westerns we'd get to watch on Sunday nights, or the more exotic African buzzards from *Wild Kingdom.* I assumed I was a goner, that the birds overhead were only doing their natural duty: indicating to the rest of the beasts in northwest Indiana that there was food to be had down below, a boy on the brink of succumbing on a pig farm just outside the outskirts of the Wabash city limits. I began to cry, a nasty, deep bawl that crescendoed and then petered out as I eased into the healthy realm of shock. Later my brothers would tell me how I took one look at the finger on ice in a baggie and went out like a bird shot from the sky. Darren read pulp fiction novels like he was competing for a world record, and while he's never confirmed this, I think his putting my finger on ice was something he'd read about in one of them.

Out on the road the tractor moved slowly, even in high gear. Darren had used the control levers near the steering wheel to tip the front scoop to the exact angle to keep me securely tilted in place as they rushed me to the county hospital. Derrick drove as Darren calmly instructed him on which lefts and rights to take. We all learned to drive early, and, while I never got their superior senses of direction, my brothers did everything they could think of to get me to the hospital quicker. At one point I came to again. I could feel the heave and bounce of the tractor, smell the hog manure wafting up from my handed-down boots. In the rush of air coming over the lip of the scoop I could hear my brother Darren trying to comfort me.

"It's OK, Dougie, it's OK," he purred. As we stopped at a four-way, I could hear Derrick sniffling, trying to hold back tears. The exhaust from the tractor was acrid but familiar, and for a moment I thought I'd actually died. The front of my overalls was crimson. I could feel my right arm shimmying and lurching at my side. The space in front of my face went white, and I was out once more.

I could tell you the details of the hospital, how the doctor sewed my finger back on using some of the skin from my plump butt, or how when I did regain consciousness all I could see for several hours were blackbirds swirling madly about me, in every one of their beaks bloody fingers, carrion of the wicked bird kind. I could tell you how the other finger, the one that had managed to dangle from a shred but had not fallen off, was cut so cleanly that it seemed minor at the time. But what I can remember the most from the hospital, after Darren and Derrick pulled the tractor up to the sliding doors of the emergency room and carried me into the lobby, one at my head, the other at my feet, like I was a Civil War soldier, were the smells of alcohol and manure as they mingled in the tiled confines of the white rooms. Our gumboots had hog shit on them, and it breached the normal medicinal smell of the emergency room. I was embarrassed by the hybrid odor we Crandells brought to the place. It smelled like an accident, I thought, as I took two huge shots of painkiller into the pulp of my fingers, the needle a pain unto itself, burning hot, the taste of vomit in my mouth before I ever lurched off the padded cot to let it spew at my feet.

But the details of the emergency room are simply not the story. My fingers would play a serious role from then on, especially that summer of 1976, when my dog Joe would find his own gore, and I would try to heal. And so I leave myself there in the emergency room with the one image that makes me feel the worst. It is of my brothers. They stood at my head, stroking my brow, Darren still hushing me with soft whispers of comfort, Derrick on the verge of bawling. When the doctor told them to hold my shoulders down, that he was about to begin sewing, snipping off the frayed skin and tucking what was left back together, Derrick cried out. It was all he could take, seeing his baby brother squirm in agony, and he ran from the room. The doctor didn't seem to notice. With determination in his brown eyes he said to Darren, "Hold your brother, son. This is going to smart."

Pillow Therapy, Rocks Too

A county sheriff had gotten in touch with my mother to inform her of the accident. My father was due back to the farm on Sunday, so she decided not to call him but rather tell him about it when he got home. I left the hospital with an enormous wad of gauze wrapped around my hand. While the nurse wound it around and around, my forearm held upright before her face, my head purely intoxicated with painkiller, I dreamed she was using my wrist and hand like a cardboard funnel, catching as much of the cotton candy gauze as she could before a bell rang.

The staff at the hospital knew our family well because we always went in the fall to get our flu shots. My mother had gotten into the habit of calling our family the 7 D's at the doctor's office too. She'd say loud and clear at the receptionist's desk, "Dan, Doris, Derrick, Dina, Darren, Doug, and Dana," when asked who was on our crappy insurance plan. When we lined up for our shot, an old nurse who most people knew was a little on the senile side would say, "Which one is Donald?" My mother would reply that it was me, that I was Donald, and the old lady with boobs down to her pockets would come at me with her syringe drawn. My mother didn't want to hurt her feelings, so for the day I'd get to be someone else. I liked it because I knew a farmer friend of my dad's named Donald, and he was tall and well respected as a self-taught vet, a midwife for pigs you might say.

As we piled into the station wagon, my mother caught a glimpse of something familiar sitting near the back entrance of the hospital. There by the dumpster was the old front-loader tractor that Darren and Derrick had driven me to the emergency room in, a striped pillow from her bed still in the manure-caked scoop. She stared at the tractor and said, "You boys are going to have to come back and get that tomorrow with your father." She didn't get into the car, just stared.

"Honey," she said to me, "go get that pillow before it gets ruined."

"I'll go get it," Darren offered, but she insisted. "No, Waynie (his middle name), let Dougie." Darren did not seem happy with the situation, but I was still high on pain medicine, and the idea of strolling across the parking lot to retrieve my mother's pillow seemed absolutely wonderful. I took my time, taking in my body's reaction to the endorphins and drugs, my legs heavy and light all at once, gold and silver etchings flashing at the farthest reaches of my vision. I reached the tractor and pulled the pillow out of the scoop. It was soaked on one end with blood. At first I couldn't register how it had gotten that way, but as I turned back toward the car, all of the other D's watching me as if I were on a tightwire walk, I felt dread wash into my stomach. I began to feel dizzy. Derrick ran to me and took the pillow. Darren put his arm around me and walked me to the car. We climbed in the rear; our station wagon had one of those back doors that opened like a hearse. My mother and the girls sat in the front. Derrick and Darren and I sat on the bench seat, facing outward. I leaned on Darren's shoulder while Derrick cradled my hand in his lap. It was warm in the car, so my mother used the main button up front to make our window go down. A cool breeze spilled into the car. Derrick rested the bloody pillow on the lip of the window, and as my mother backed up it fell out onto the pavement. Darren yelled "Whoa!" and my mother braked. Derrick carefully passed my wadded hand to Darren and bent out the window. He snatched the pillow from the ground. It started to sprinkle rain as he pulled himself back into the car. My mother flipped the button up front to roll up the windows and caught him as the window rose. It wedged him across his belly. He yelled in protest as my mother fiddled with the switch to get the window back down. After a couple of seconds, he was back inside the car with the bloody pillow. Darren started laughing first, then Derrick. The girls and my mother started, and then finally I let myself give in as well. Outside, the rain fell harder. We backed out of the parking lot, the car filled with laughter. While my mother put the car in drive I watched, as the neon emergency sign got blurry. We were leaving it behind, but in that backseat, facing the opposite direction, it seemed like we'd just arrived.

The doctors at the hospital were concerned that a staph infection might develop in my fingers from the manure and to counteract the chance, the hospital sent me home with large jugs of antibacterial solution the color of rust. My mother read the instructions aloud as we all sat around the table that Saturday night. She wanted to have a full and competent grasp on how to heal me so that she could settle everyone in the family down. Dina and Dana had been crying off and on, asking me if I could feel anything, or if the stitches were made of horsehair.

Although I was somewhat relieved to escape the tortuous summer regime of farm work, I had to figure out how I was going to do things one-handed. The hand that had borne the burden of brushing teeth, turning pages, driving tractors, and feeding livestock was useless. Worse, it had to be soaked twice a day in a tray of water saturated with Epsom salts. This was not a pleasant experience. The stitches—fifteen on one finger, ten on the other (a lot for fingers only as big around as pencils)—stuck to the gauze bandages, and the salve the doctor gave my mother to put on them smelled weird, like mold or sulfur or the water left over from boiled hotdogs. And then there was the way my fingers looked: ugly and red, like roadkill innards.

Even now, all these years later, the middle one has a bunk-bed nail: one up top, stubby and close to the cuticle, and another below, ridged and cracked, with the appearance, if I let it grow, of a dewclaw. A pale, raised scar rings the deformed area just below the last knuckle, circling my finger like a fishing worm just under the skin.

My head was clearing up and before nightfall I would have to be given another pain pill from a bottle that matched the color of the cleaning solution in the jugs at my mother's feet. While she read, mostly directing herself to Darren, who sat next to me scribbling down notes, I imagined my hand under the bandages. Up until then, I'd not seen, up close anyway, much in the way of dead animals. I was not yet allowed in the farrowing house and if any of our older sows died, the stink wagon was there before long to haul them away. But I was aware that dead things made maggots, that in order for something to be really dead it had to lie around while the worms magically appeared from within, telling whoever looked that it was true, yes, this thing is dead. I thought under my bandages the same would happen. Soon, I thought, the maggots would be wiggling around my stitches, squirming their way down my fingers to the meaty base for more food. My mother finished reading the aftercare orders.

"When will the maggots get in there?" Dana asked, pointing to my hand. She'd come to the same conclusion I had. My mother looked to Darren.

"There isn't going to be any," he said. He kicked the jugs under the table. "This stuff will keep them extra clean, and besides, Doug's not dead. You'd have to be dead for that." My mother went to the sink and started washing dishes. My little sister Dana spoke up again, stubborn as a plow in mud. "Well, his fingers are dead. They might come then."

Darren got a little angry. All five of us kids sat around the table, willing to talk the accident through. "No," he said fiercely. "Dougie's fingers aren't dead. They're cut up bad, but the doctor fixed them. I saw it."

"That stupid auger bin," my little sister said. "We ought to hurt it." We had moved into the debriefing stage. My mother remained at the sink, thinking, banging pots, very distracted. Of course, I knew the doctor's bill would set back my parents' dream once again. They'd have to use what they'd saved to pay for the emergency room visit, rolls and rolls of gauze over the summer, and before it was over we'd probably spend enough on Epsom salts alone to own stock in the company. I watched her at the sink, her back to us, her right arm going counterclockwise very slowly, drying a dinner plate. It gleamed in the fluorescent light. Dana wanted to punish the auger. She said again, "We oughta give that bin away."

"We can't, silly," Derrick said solemnly. "It's not even ours." I thought I saw my mother flinch at his comment; she nearly dropped the plate, but she didn't turn around. Darren spoke. "None of us should go near that bin again. None of us." His voice gave way a bit, a thickness in his words made him sound older.

My mother twisted quickly from the sink. She said, louder than we'd been talking, "Come on, put on your boots. We're going out there now. You need to see it's just a piece of farm machinery."

We all stared up at her like she was losing it. Darren started to speak but she cut him off. "No, now let's go out there and get this over with." It was more of her tough love, like the hospital parking lot and the pillow fetch. Strangely enough, I was the first to pull on my gumboots. I wanted to see where the accident had happened. I thought it was a good idea and told my mother so as the six of us walked toward the barn lot, the swallows dipping down out of the murky dusk to feast on the insects swarming under the utility lights.

We stood back from the auger in a line, biggest to smallest, our mother chewing gum and snapping it lightly. We stared at the structure for some time; it was like seeing the outline of a mountain way off in the distance, before light had fully come up. Darren reached down and picked up a rock. He broke free of the line and turned to hand it to me.

"Throw it," he said, pointing to the enormous cone tower. Now the bin appeared to me like some medieval castle in the fading light, its shadow engulfing us, turning everyone's face sepia. I took the stone and felt its sharp flints in my palm. I am right-handed, the hand that now was only a ball of white. I wound up my left arm and threw the stone toward the bin with all my might. It fell very short of the target, landing just a few feet in front of us. Derrick picked it up and gave it to me again. Dana yelled, "Hit that dumb old thing, Dougie!" I used a different turn of the wrist and heaved the rock again. It went a little farther. "Yeah!" yelled my sisters, as they clapped and egged me on. "Try another one!"

"Help me," I told them. One by one they all stooped to find a rock. Darren took control of the activity, smiling broadly.

He counted off loudly. "One...two...three." The rocks sailed forth. Only my mother's and Darren's and Derrick's made contact. It was nearly dark by now. The sound of the rocks hitting the metal bin made a rapid-fire clatter, solid thuds in the dark. Darren took me by the arm and walked me to the bin, careful not to let me fall. When we were close enough to touch the bin he gave me another stone. He told me, "Throw it at the bottom, Dougie." I hauled off and slammed the rock down with all the might my awkward left arm could muster. It bashed hard against the metal; a cracking sound rang out. Cheers rose up. Darren escorted me back to the others, telling me how great I'd done. Out of nowhere Joe came pouncing up, his hot breath at our shins, the furry trace of his tail tickling our faces as we bent to pet him. Darren had taught him to sit, and also to howl when Darren would imitate the sound of a coyote. Dana told Joe to sit. He ignored her, leaped around us in the dark, yapping as if he'd treed something and was trying to tell us where it was.

Dana told Joe again to sit. His eyes on her face, he obeyed this time, scooting up to us, all hyper on his haunches, waiting for Darren to begin. He cleared his voice and howled the coyote sound, his neck thrown back, lips pursed. Joe didn't respond. His head was turned away, not paying attention. Darren waved his hand to get the dog's attention. Joe locked his gaze on Darren's face and sat stone-still. Darren howled to the sky and Joe began to croon along with him, their combined song horrible as metal grinding steel. For some reason, maybe because I'd just let myself start thinking about my fingers again, I started to cry. Darren and Joe drowned me out, though, and I let go, knowing I could get away with it. In the dark I let my fear all out. I was grateful for my family around me, who'd helped me do it so soon.

First Soaks During Hee Haw

$\textbf{M}$y father pulled into the drive shortly after we'd cleared the table, putting our bowls of stray Wheaties and gray milk into the sink one by one, each of us passing them up to Derrick, who stood dumping the milk into the drain. Our mother had asked us to give her some time with our dad on the porch before we came out. It was a warm morning. The panes of glass in the kitchen windows made shiny reflections over our heads. We all peeked out the window, watching my mother tell our dad about the accident. I was ashamed. I thought I'd done a dumb thing. Of course, I had. We watched them that way for several minutes. My dad shook his head, using the edge of the concrete porch to skim the mud from his boots. They hugged. We ran to sit around the kitchen table. My dad opened the kitchen door slowly and walked in. I'd placed my gauzy hand on the table for easy viewing. The others stared at it there.

"You OK, son?" he asked. I nodded yes. "Well then, let's get you all dressed for chores." He walked back outside and lit a cigarette, offered a drag to my mother. She mouthed "no thanks" to him. As we filed out of the room, Darren said, "Dougie, let me help you with your overalls."

With my grandparents away, it was as if we had two houses, and two farms. Something in my parents eased. The tension they felt with my dad's parents always within earshot seemed to melt away. That first day after my accident was palpably relaxed. We worked together as a family, performing the chores and eating our meals in leisure. While I certainly wasn't able to be much help, it was comforting to see that things went on as usual, that my fingers hadn't triggered a complete collapse of the farm. As it got closer and closer to dark, though, after we'd fed everything that needed feeding, I became scared. I knew that at nighttime doctor's orders were to remove the bandages and soak my fingers in a warm tray of Epsom salts. As we walked to the house, my parents arm-in-arm, I felt like running away into the field or climbing into the haymow to crawl inside the intricate maze of straw tunnels to escape the inevitable.

We were all on the steps removing our boots when a gunshot rang out, echoing off the cement silos. We jumped, and all of us kids ran to the end of the porch to see where the shot had come from. My father ordered us inside, and we went halfheartedly with my mother. Normally, gunfire meant nothing more than a neighbor shooting at some feral dogs, or scaring off a flock of disease-carrying pigeons (whose crap could kill a litter of pigs in nothing flat). Lately, though, our farm had somehow become a stop off for prisoners escaping from the county farm. In less than a year, two criminals had fled while on ditch duty inside the city limits and headed across our field lickety-split, trying to run over the deep furrows before they were noticed missing. One night when my dad was in the fields, a county sheriff and his deputy flew overhead in a helicopter, shining a bright searchlight down on our buildings, commanding us from the sky to stay put inside, that a criminal was hiding on our farm. So instead of wondering which neighbor was shooting at a pack of dogs, we assumed the shot was a sign that another inmate had made a break for it across the field, heading to our farm to hide in the pasture or sleep with the sows.

We crowded at the windows, trying to see out the back. My mother ordered the others to be careful. "Watch it! You're going to bump up against Dougie's hand!" I didn't want to hear that kind of thing. I was already tired of feeling that I couldn't do what everyone else could. It was going to be a long summer. I eased back so they could look without getting in trouble. Outside, another shot fired, quick and loud. Darren said, "That sounded like a .22 rifle."

"Ooh," Dana said, as if she knew what it meant. My mother told the others to get away from the windows, that for all we knew there could be some convict out there. I wondered why, then, she didn't seemed too concerned for my dad. As if she knew what I was thinking, she said, "Your dad will be all right. I am sure it's just Old Man Enyeart shooting at that hound that's been killing his chickens."

We all sat down at the kitchen table and didn't speak a word, afraid that we might miss hearing another shot. I was as excited as on the days school was delayed or sometimes canceled altogether because of fog. Those mornings were perfect. The sun would come out and burn off the low-lying fog by eleven A.M. and we would have the rest of the day to partake in odd chores we never saw performed any other time. Tilling the ground around the sheds so rye could be sowed for birds (so they'd be attracted to the barns to eat lice) or power-washing the farm implements with an anti-rust spray or running wire just a foot off the ground to keep the sows from invading certain parts of the lot; these were all duties that took on a carefree air in the hours thieved from school. "Thank God for fog," Darren would say as he screwed around in a shed with some contraption he was trying to make. Once he welded a cane for my grandmother, fashioned it out of steel. She told everyone he was going to be president of the United States one day; she'd say those exact words. The cane was so heavy she could barely lift it. But since it was made by a future occupant of the Oval Office, she dragged the metal cane from her front porch to the garden without a second thought, stopping every few feet to take a breather.

Now I felt the same giddiness come over me as with the fog days. I dreaded the idea of unwrapping my fingers and soaking them. It was as if I had to face the accident over and over again. If there was a man on the loose in our field, heading our way with a gun, at least I wouldn't have to undress my fingers, the fingers I'd already accepted were going to be uglier than just about anything on the farm.

I closed my eyes when I heard my dad on the porch, realizing that my hope of postponing the soaking was dying with every clop of his foot. He burst into the kitchen, red-faced and angry.

"That damn dog is going to get himself killed wandering onto other people's farms," he said, going to the sink for a drink. He filled a glass to the brim, lifted it to his lips, and sucked it down. He ripped a loud and gravelly belch and turned to address us at the table. "Darren, I thought we talked about that dog. You boys need to keep an eye on him."

"Why?" Darren asked. "What happened?"

"He was over on Mr. Higgly's place. Chasing his shoats. He didn't do anything, but Higgly shot in the air to scare him off. I can't find him out there at all." Our dad turned to fill his glass once more at the sink, and said, "Isn't it time to get Doug's fingers doctored?" I felt myself tense. I knew better than to try and fight it, and steeled my mind for what I might see.

The water was too hot at first to even think about putting my hand in. My mother blew on it as Darren sat at my side with his book open. I watched as my mother placed a towel out on the table. "Put your hand up here, Dougie," she said. She wielded a pair of stub-nosed surgical scissors the doctor had sent home with us. I was to soak my fingers for fifteen minutes in the water, then let them air dry, and afterward apply some of the gross-looking solution to them, bandage them up, and do it all again in the morning.

My mother cut a slit in the gauze and removed several of the outer layers of cotton padding, careful to remember how it all was to go back on. My dad and the other kids were watching TV, *Hee Haw,* to be exact, a show my father thought was the best damn program on television. I could hear Minnie Pearl telling a joke. I imagined the price tag on her hat swaying as she popped up from the fake cornfield backdrop to deliver her one-line zinger.

Naked, my fingers looked like hamburger meat with black string ground in; the stitches appeared haphazardly sewn, twisted and stiff. Darren waited for my mother to pull my hand into the water and began reading to me from one of the paperbacks he seemed to devour by the dozen. He'd planned for everything. If my attention started to fade away from the book, he'd brought to the table a Donald Duck figurine, elastic string in its limbs, able to perform a dance. If you pushed the button on the bottom, Donald would go limp all over, and when you released it, he'd shoot back to attention, erect in his little blue-and-white sailor uniform, yellow bowtie at his throat, another, smaller, on the brim of his cap. Darren read out loud as I put Donald Duck in my mouth and chewed. The story was about two mob men up to their chins in stolen money; it took place somewhere on an island and the cover had a treasure chest on it with gold coins dripping with blood.

The briny water felt like a thousand needles sticking into the rawness of my fingers. I bit down hard on Donald, my misshapen teeth pushing at the base as his limbs went limp, springing back into shape as I released my choppers. Over and over the figurine went from lifeless and wilted to alive and firm as I continued to chomp on the toy, Darren holding my other hand, reading quicker and more pronounced as I winced. The fifteen minutes seemed like an eternity. With a sweaty brow and my teeth aching from Donald, it was finally over. My mother pulled my hand from the water and put it again on a clean dishtowel. I got a good look at it then, bare, in the open air without the curtain of gauze to keep me from seeing the entire horror show. The stitches were long, some of the ends sticking up like cowlicks, and under them little nodules of tissue poked out, cinched tightly, ridged and tinged with maroon. I stared at the hand as if it weren't mine, like it had been totally dismembered from my body and put on display before being bagged for disposal. I think I might have slipped back into some shock then. I tried to move the fingers but couldn't; they remained still as the others twitched.

"Don't," my mother said, dabbing them with solution. "Let them rest." Darren read some more to me that night at the table, even after my fingers were all bandaged up. I could hear the final silliness on *Hee Haw,* the part he liked the most. Buck Owens, apickin' and agrinnin'. I loved Darren at that moment as deeply as a person could. I'd always been a child to give hugs and kisses without much provocation, and sitting there with my brother I couldn't resist the urge to lean toward him and kiss him on his soft cheek. I left my lips there for a long time, my good arm and hand around his neck, him reading on and on about a bad guy who was the best hit man the mob had ever known.

A Glimpse of Jimmy

3

With my grandpa gone, I was eager to get to see inside the farrowing house. We had a bumper crop of baby pigs every few months, and during the night my dad had gotten up several times to check on the sows. In the morning, I tried to pull on my boots to go to my grandparents' farm across the pasture to get a peek at what was going on, but my mother stopped me, saying, "Dougie, you can't take your fingers in there. They'll get infected." I tried to argue but she wouldn't listen. Finally she said, "Maybe in a couple days you can go in there. The piglets will still be coming then."

I had to stay in the house as Derrick and Darren and my dad went to the farrowing house and my mother and the girls tried a new recipe for bundt cake for the fair taking place in just a couple of months. Bored, I went into the bathroom, one of my favorite activities, to look around at what my mother had done to it. As soon as the Bicentennial year had arrived, she decorated the room with red, white, and blue paint, gold stars, and silver

51

glitter. One night before my accident she told all of us kids to come and help her. She'd painted a section of wall by the sink with red paint. It was still wet when she passed around the plastic bag of glitter to us. "Take a good handful, now," she said proudly, smiling as if about to show us a card trick she'd learned.

"Now come here to the wall, kids." We followed her, clinching our fists tightly so the glitter wouldn't escape. She asked Darren to count down from ten. When he got to zero, we tossed the glitter at the wall. Most of it fell short, but my mother's handful and Derrick's stuck to the wall in perfect bursts of twinkling chrome. "Just like a fireworks in the sky," my mother said, as we all scurried to get another handful. It was great fun and by the time she had finished that section of wall it was transformed into a shrine of Independence, replete with flag decals on the side of the tub and a fuzzy, stars-and-stripes toilet seat cover. She still had a good three-fourths of the bathroom to finish, but her start on it was impressive.

I liked picking the glitter off, inspecting the pocks in the paint underneath, imagining I'd discover something special there. My mother had convened several meetings with us kids to inquire about who was doing the picking. I never confessed and kept right on with my secret work until she redid the bathroom again in 1977.

I was mad that I could not go with the men to the farrowing house, and took it out on the wall. I used a metal fingernail file to really dig into the globs of glitter. I'd scraped off the biggest area so far when my mother knocked on the door. "Dougie, do you want to come help us with the baking?" I dropped the file into the wastebasket and pretended to flush the toilet. "No, thank you," I said. "I'm going to watch some TV." My mother said, "OK," and I could hear her leave the door. I left the bathroom, carrying my hand upright like the doctor had told me to. He said it would help with the healing if the blood flowed in both directions. "Let it hang like you normally would half the day, and the other half carry it like you're holding a protest sign." I preferred holding it up. When it hung at my side the pain was worse. The four magic pills that made me feel like an angel hovering over the farm from above, counting each and every little piggy and the hairs on their chinny-chin-chins as well, had been used already. I was on my own now, straight. I'd have to learn to tolerate the alternating dull aches and sharp pangs in my fingers by biting on a washcloth or nipping the inside of my cheek until it bled.

I switched on the television and rotated the clunky dial around the horn, each click producing another out-of-focus picture until I used the looser circle of plastic inside the dial to fine-tune it. No cartoons. I left the TV on and went to the couch to sit. I'd never watched the news, hadn't been allowed to, really. An anchorman said they'd be right back with an in-depth look at a peanut farmer from Georgia who was running for president. I locked my eyes onto the TV. All I'd heard was the word *farmer,* followed by *president.* I knew some men who farmed who sat on the Wabash County School Board and a pig farmer who was a circuit court judge part-time, but this, this was big news. Maybe Darren really would become president. Maybe someday a newsman would be saying how they'd return after a couple of commercial breaks to interview a hog farmer from Indiana who was running for president. I concentrated on the television set, goose bumps up and down my arms.

I slid down from the couch and sat before the TV on the carpet. I moved the bunny ears on top to make the picture as clear as I knew how. The newsman returned to the screen. He wore a suit jacket with a lapel to his shoulders and a necktie as wide as the blue shirt beneath. The footage of the peanut farmer came on. I couldn't believe his name was Jimmy, like a kid. They showed him in a red clay field in Plains, Georgia, walking between rows of peanut plants. I was astonished that peanuts didn't grow on trees. Jimmy plucked a plant from the ground, the knobby peanuts dangling with dirt from the roots. He had a smile that I wanted, his teeth broad and white, straight and sweet looking as he shook the plant free of soil, popping a peanut, hull and all, into his mouth. Something else stood out about Jimmy that struck me as quite fine. He had blond hair. No one else in my family had it, just me, and the fact that Jimmy, a farmer in a denim shirt and blue jeans, had blond hair like mine made me feel like we were secretly related. The TV lit up with scenes from his childhood. His full name was James Earl Carter. I liked that. I repeated his name out loud, then my own: Doug Eugene Crandell. It was close. Maybe my grandmother had been wrong, maybe it was me who'd be president, not Darren. Or maybe Darren would make it first, then I'd follow. I was a little let down when the narrator said Jimmy had been thin all his life, not chunky like me. I didn't let it stop me from scooting closer to the TV, though, my hand upright, carrying an imaginary vote-for-Jimmy sign.

The news piece ended way too soon. The screen showed where each county's political party's office was. In block letters it read Wabash County Democratic Headquarters. I knew where that was. I remembered from all the field trips that the court-house and lightbulb shrine were close by. After the information disappeared, an ad came on. It showed Jimmy standing in his farm field with the same denim clothes on. A flag flew on a pole in downtown Plains, Georgia, as Jimmy walked up some steps. I felt ashamed that I'd messed with my mother's bathroom walls when they showed him pledging allegiance, red, white, and blue swarming in all directions. I stood and held the beehive of gauze over my heart. A boy who'd do such a thing wouldn't make it to the Opal Office, a term I'd misheard and couldn't get right over the next few months. When the ad was over I shut off the TV. I could hear my sisters and mother in the kitchen talking about the cake they were making, how good it would be to eat right out of the oven. My shame had turned to a sense of duty as I walked quietly to the bathroom, the way I'd seen Jimmy walk, with his chin up but smiling too, confident and gentle.

I closed the bathroom door and locked it, fished the nail file out of the trash, and put it back inside the medicine cabinet. With one hand I got to work. I unscrewed some red nail polish of my mother's and painted generous swabs of it in the areas I'd picked. I found the bag of silver glitter under the sink; there was only a little bit left, but I knew I could make it work. After all, farmers were leaders and could make do with what they had. Peanuts, glitter, hogs, whatever, Jimmy and I were cut from the same cloth, and I had the blond hair to prove it. Carefully, diligently, I restored all the patches I'd defaced. When I was through I went to the kitchen and told my mother I'd fixed the spots in the bathroom. We'd learned in school that George Washington could not tell a lie. I hadn't heard what Jimmy couldn't do, but I was certain he didn't lack a thing. My mother hugged me. With batter and flour on her hands, she held them upright to keep from getting any in my blond presidential hair.

And Then There Were Two

9

That Darren might have a competitor for the office, or a potential running mate, I kept to myself. I had a diary and scrawled in it the best I could the address of the county's democratic headquarters. I planned on getting there somehow, but for now my sights were set on the farrowing house. If I was going to use farming as my platform, like Jimmy, I'd have to change from Pig Boy to something more dignified. With Darren's help, I was able to convince my parents to let me inside during the next day's rounds. Darren insisted that my hand would be fine. He would personally see to it by using three empty bread bags, tying them tightly over my hand to keep out any potential infection. He used jute rope to cinch the three-ply bags. It was bulky, uncomfortable, and silly looking, but I didn't care. With my grandparents in Terre Haute for only a week I knew I had to move quickly, and by the time Darren got done telling me how great it was inside the farrowing house, I was willing to promise anything to get inside.

That night he told me stories of what it was like in there.

"You wouldn't believe all the piglets. Some of the sows have had twenty babies or more, and there's so many colors they look like calico kittens." We slept in the same bed, the three boys, and at night, with a cowhide over us that I thought was fake but was actually from Darren's first 4-H steer, he would let me in on some of farm life's great and enduring secrets, while Derrick snored away in a deep sleep.

I begged him to tell me more. "Well, with all the babies out now, we counted over 200. Tomorrow, Dad says we're going to give them all their shots and dock their tales. They're so soft and warm. You can hold some if you want. Grandpa isn't here to get onto us."

I didn't like the thought of the piglets having their tails cut off. I knew what it was like to have something chopped off. I felt I was sinking into the bed, down through the coils to the frame underneath, never to get the chance to hold the babies in a building that represented to me a secret I'd never be told. Darren detected the reason for my silence. It was common knowledge that I was a sensitive child with an overactive imagination. I'd already gotten into my head that some farm animals, particularly our neighbors' beef cattle, could walk on their hind legs like people, using their hooves to open doors and come after those who wanted to butcher them. Often when the neighbors' Hereford cattle escaped the barbed wire or slipped over a low place in the fence and proceeded up our lane, visible from the front porch, I would run into the house and begin piling footstools and houseplants before the door, certain at any moment that the cattle would stand up and saunter into our house prepared to exact their revenge.

Now, in the dark bedroom, I couldn't find the words to tell him how wrong it would be to cut off the babies' tails. I could feel the blood pulsing through the skinned carcass of my fingers.

"Dougie?" I didn't answer. He sat up in the bed and told me to scoot toward him. He patted his chest in the dark, which meant I was to put my head there. He let me rest on him when I was sick or needed to calm down from the many nightmares I sweated through. I put my head against his bare skin. I tried to make his heartbeat match the thumping in my fingers. Swoosh, swoosh, swoosh. His blood pumped fast and hard under his bony sternum. I lifted my head when he began to speak.

"The thing is, those little guys don't feel that much. I've done it, and you know I wouldn't do it if it hurt them."

"Why do their tails have to come off?" I asked. He took a deep breath. I put my head back down on his chest, snuggled up to him, listening to the crystal sound of his voice, so smart and measured, so completely soothing to anything painful. He brushed my forehead with his hand, pushing my damp bangs out of my eyes.

"Well," he started. "They just can't have them when they are all together, that's all." I didn't understand what he meant.

"'Cause why?"

"They fight over them if their tails are long. So it's best that we take them off when they're little and can't feel it." His lungs skipped an intake; he sputtered as he tried to compensate. Darren had constant bronchitis, untreated because it would mean more medical bills. Our family always said he talked too fast, that he got ahead of himself in everything, even breathing, so eager was he to get things done.

I asked again why the pigs had to lose their tails. He said, "Hmmmm," and then started to speak more slowly.

"See, if we didn't do it now, they'd get their tails slammed in car doors and tangled up in fences and stuff." I giggled, not knowing for sure if he was serious or telling me a silly story. He said, "Once I heard about a sow without her tail docked, and she got it wrapped around another pig's mouth. They were wild pigs,

you know, like those ones we saw in the river bottom that time."
I felt my eyes getting heavier. The pain in my hand drifted off as
Darren continued on with the story, scooting down in the bed to
get comfortable, my head and body going with him.

"So they were like elephants in a circus, the way they held
each other's tails with their trunks. But the sow that had its nose
roped with the other one's tail couldn't eat or drink. She started
to get skinny, which was good, 'cause she was one of the Chester
Whites that get real fat. Anyway, the sow in front took good care
of the one behind her until..." He stopped telling the story, thinking I had fallen asleep. I nudged him for more, but he didn't
respond.

"Then what happened?" I asked.

"Nothing." He thought for a moment. "Nothing you want to
know." I was intrigued. "Tell me," I pleaded. "Please."

"OK, but don't get all mad about it, OK?" I agreed. "The thing
is, that sow behind the other couldn't stand not eating, so she..."

"What?"

"She got ahold of that tail, nipping at it and using her tongue
to pull it in her mouth until she took a big bite out of it. She
docked that other sow's tail for her."

I'd promised not to overreact, to behave more like a grown-
up hog man than a little chubby pig boy, so I remained quiet. It
was difficult, but I started to drift off again while Darren changed
the subject and talked about the baby pigs again. Right before I
went to sleep he said, "Dougie, we have to take their tails off. It's
for their own good. You understand?" I was exhausted, and simply mumbled that I did understand, even though I didn't and
was merely intoxicated from dozing. I am sure he meant to use
the timing that way, to try and get me to accept a more mature
approach to the realities of pig farming. Later I'd find out just
why pigs in close proximity were better off without their tails—

pigs are carnivores and will eat anything—but that night I fell asleep without pestering him anymore about it. Which was exactly how he'd planned it.

My mind sorted through awful dreams during the early hours of the night. I saw pigs with no tails, hogs with my nasty fingers stuck to their butts in place of tails, and little pigs with tails for ears and tongues and umbilical cords that served as wild grappling limbs attached to their sides like wings. When the light hit me in the face, beaming down from the square fixture on the bedroom ceiling, I thought I was having another dream about the emergency room, re-creating in my sleep how the floodlights had nearly blinded me as the doctor sewed my fingers back together.

When Darren shook me by the shoulders I came to more, and realized my father was standing at the bedroom door, dressed in work clothes, telling us to get up, that our mother was sick. She was in the bathroom now, he said, but he needed us to help.

Just four days after I went to the hospital, my mother had to go to the emergency room, too. We got up and dressed in our chore clothes. My dad had left us to go knock on the bathroom door to see if my mother was OK. We could hear him saying, "Doris? Doris? You OK?" as we pulled on our overalls, tucking the cuffs into knee-high gumboots. Derrick was already up helping my father in the farrowing house with a sow who couldn't get her babies to come out. When my dad had come into the house to get more rubbing alcohol for the sow, he'd found my mother throwing up in the sink.

My hand was aching horribly under the gauze, feeling like a cramped muscle with a bad burnt place on top. I followed Darren downstairs. My father knocked once more on the bathroom door and when there was no answer he burst in, telling us to stay out, but we peeked in anyway. My mom had passed out on the floor.

61

The front of her nightgown was covered with blood. She moaned, writhing on the tile like she was dying, which I assumed she was.

My dad scooped her up in his arms and stormed past us. "Darren! Go get the car and pull it up front to the porch!" In a flash, Darren grabbed the keys and flew out the front door into the blackness of the early morning. I watched the headlights through the tall panes of glass in the living room. They cut a swath of yellow across the walnut trees in the front yard as he sped around the circle drive and got the station wagon so close to the porch that he had trouble getting out. My mother started to weep. I held the bloody tip of her nightgown as it dangled from her legs. My father's eyes were wild with worry, but he tried to tell her it was going to be fine.

"You're OK, Dory. You're OK," he repeated again and again. Darren came back into the house and held the door open for my father. "What's wrong with her, Dad?" he asked.

"I don't know. She's fine, though." By now, Dina and Dana had heard the noise and come downstairs. They stood squinting, holding hands, crying before they'd even seen the blood. My mother sobbed. "I'm sorry," she repeated every time my father insisted she was going to be all right.

Before he carried our mother out the door to the car, my father told Darren to get out to the farrowing house to help Derrick. "That black sow is bundled up again with pigs. You girls stay inside." He left. In one smooth action he was behind the wheel, my mother leaning into his lap as he steered the car down the lane and out onto Pike Street. We watched the red lights until they disappeared. I imagined them passing the city limits sign and traveling quickly through the dark morning to the hospital. I pressed my face against the window, Dana by my side, sniffling, still half asleep. "What's wrong with Mommy?" Darren stepped to the window and guided us both to the sofa. Dina couldn't move from the foot of the stairs.

Darren seemed to want to tell us something else, but couldn't make the words form in his mouth. He puckered and blew, empty vowel sounds dying before he could go on. It was the first time I'd seen him truly scared. He stood up and told me to come with him.

"Girls," he said. "When we get back from the chores it would be nice to have pancakes and bacon." He smiled. Dina stepped forward and rubbed away her tears. She sucked up the wetness below her nose. She took Dana's hand.

"OK, Darren. We can do it. Can't we, Dana?" We were all pleased to have familiar work to occupy our minds. Later, after my mother had been admitted to the hospital for an emergency hysterectomy, our dad would tell us that we needed to really help out for the next few weeks as she recovered. I thought the word was *lobotomy*, a term I'd heard used in a horror movie. I looked it up and thought our mother had had part of her brain taken out. Instead, a large cyst had burst inside her, described to us by our father in terms that seemed to border on the fantastic. "A bubble inside her woman parts blew up. She'll be fine."

Of course, at the time we were keenly aware, as we had been just days earlier with my accident, that our dream of owning our own farm would again be delayed. Just like farm equipment breakdowns, our bodies held the potential for disaster. A broken arm, severed appendage, concussion, even a common cold signaled a reason for alarm. It meant setback and frustration. Early on we started to mirror our parents' attitude when it came to our health. We didn't talk about feeling sick or mention injuries. We refused to have our temperatures taken and hid significant cuts that really needed stitches, opting to treat our wounds with store-bought bandages instead. Our grandparents had been in mediocre health, but regular doctor visits without health insurance took its toll on the down payment money my mother tracked weekly at the kitchen table. We were young and sturdy; the money, if it had to be used for the doctor, was meant for our grandparents. Our parents had never said so, had not once told us to do without or ignore aches and pains and injury, but they'd modeled it. Once on a visit to a friend's cattle farm on a Sunday afternoon my father was bitten badly by the man's dog. But instead of heading straight to the emergency room, he literally acted as if it hadn't happened. Even as the dog sank its sharp teeth into the back of his calf, shaking wildly as if throttling prey to death, my dad pretended not to notice. He just shooed the dog away, saying, "Get outta here, dog. Get!" The owner pulled the dog off our dad's leg, but not before the bitch had laid his leg open good, a hunk of pale skin dangling as he walked, framed by a larger tear in his jeans. My mother tried to talk him into seeing the doctor, but he said, "Ah, that's nothing but a scratch."

I could barely contain my excitement at the door to the farrowing house, a spot where I'd pressed the side of my head hard against the door so many times, I believed my earprint would give me away. Darren gave me last-minute instructions on how to behave. I was to keep my bread-bagged hand nowhere near the crate doors; a smash between one of them would ruin my fingers for good. Also, I could pet the baby pigs with my left hand but had to keep the injured hand behind my back when I played with the babies. Up until right then, I'd only been allowed in the building when it was nearly empty.

Other than the time my grandfather stole my baby pigs away, I'd only seen one litter of pigs up close. That was only because the sow had somehow been impregnated by a rogue boar that escaped from another farmer's pasture and disappeared after he'd done the deed. The pigs were small and all white, and they were moved before I got a chance to hold any of them. The real piglet bounty, I knew, was right inside the door.

I could hear soft little squeals and hooves pattering the crate floors. Darren took me by the shoulders sternly. "If you get hurt in here, or get upset, you know what will happen. If Grandpa finds out when he gets back that we let you come in, he'll be mad enough. Don't make it worse."

I shook my head thoroughly to make sure he knew I was going to act right. We were worried about my mother for sure, which is why we were throwing ourselves so much into the work, but this was exciting stuff. When we'd left the house the girls were already planning the big breakfast, the kitchen in a haze of flour as they mixed, baked, and cooked. If we could focus on the work, then we'd find out how our mother was doing soon enough. For me, the excitement was a guilty pleasure. I told myself I would be helping my mother by taking care of the baby pigs. They would get the care I couldn't give to her.

I stepped into the farrowing house slowly. Darren told me to stay near the end while he and Derrick turned the rest of the sows out for their morning exercise and feeding. There was an aisle down the center of the floor where the sows could walk to a rear door to be turned out into a large pasture. Some of the sows were so used to having babies in the building that they could open the door with their snouts.

Darren and Derrick ushered the last of the twenty sows out as I waited impatiently at the other end of the building. A red glow hung over the stalls, infrared light coming off the heating lamps that kept the babies warm while their mamas were out stretching their legs. Darren motioned for me to walk forward. The building was filled with the sounds of baby pigs: little grunts, faint oinking, and the ruckus of siblings chasing one another.

I held my hand above my head and took solid steps toward my brothers. Darren told me to walk carefully. The floor was slick. They both held trays in their hands full of syringes, swabs, rubbing alcohol, vials of antibiotic, and some tools that looked as though they could be used to dock little tails.

"I put a litter of pigs down here," Darren said, motioning behind him. "They've all been treated, so you can play with them." I shifted my feet quickly, wanting to get past him so I could get started. He became stern again. "Dougie, you're gonna hear some squeals when we take care of the others, OK? You just stay in the crate with the litter and we'll be done before long."

Darren put his tray on top of a crate and took me by the arm. He relaxed as he walked me to the litter of babies I was going to get to play with. "Guess how many are in there?" he said. I couldn't see over the railing. I smiled excitedly.

"Ten?"

"Nope."

"Thirteen?"

"Nope." He looked excited, too. "There are twenty-two pigs in there."

He opened the crate door and helped me climb in. A mass of color scurried to the far corner of the stall and huddled under the red heating lamp. It smelled like puppies. The crate was wide and warm, the floor clean and smooth.

"Now, remember," Darren said, pointing to my hand. He gave me a burlap bag. "That's vitamin pellets. They love the taste. Just sit down and let them get used to you and they'll eat right out of your hand." He closed the door, pausing for a metal click before turning to leave. As he walked away, he said louder, "If you need something, flip that heating lamp switch off and on again. I'll see it." It had been just five days since he trusted me with the auger switch, and I was determined not to cause any more trouble now, but the thought of touching another electrical switch was enough to make me feel nauseous.

I sat down slowly on the floor. My legs stuck out like I was about to play a game of roll-the-ball. The little pigs crammed themselves into a mound, climbing over each other in an attempt to hide from the stocky boy with one hand bundled like white bread sitting in their crib. The litter was just two days old. I could see their stubby tails, and the thin, almost translucent scabs covering the tips where they'd been docked. I decided to put it out of my mind. I shook the bag of pellets lightly, trying to coax them from the corner. I couldn't see their colors too well; the red light made them all appear bronzed, like the small animal statues on a shelf in the library at school. I reached deep into the bag, holding it to my chest with my right arm, keeping the hand clear of danger, and pulled out a left-handed clutch of the feed. I sprinkled the pellets between my feet, trailing it up toward the V of my legs.

The sound of the pellets hitting the floor made the baby pigs freeze stone-still, their eyes fixed to the right, listening for something else. One by one the little pigs sniffed the air. They took cautious steps forward, noses wet and twitching. As they left the artificial light I could see that the entire litter was of the same color and pattern. The undercoat was a deep red-brown, with black ovals covering their backs and sides. They looked like leopard cubs as each one bravely stepped inside my outstretched legs to snatch a pellet. My hand was sticky and smelled like molasses. The vitamins were coated in syrup to make them more appealing to the baby pigs, and by all indications the trick worked. Each pig would suck up its treat and head for the corner to nibble on it, then return to me to try for another. In just a few seconds the pellets were gone.

I reached in again and grabbed less than before. I wanted to make the feeding last as long as possible. I put my hand out in front of me. The biggest piglet of the litter inched forward and stole a pellet so quickly all I felt was a quick damp dab on my palm from his cold nose. Slowly, the other piglets came forward to eat. I put some of the feed around my legs. They nibbled on the pellets from all sides. I could see their soft little bodies whisk by my thigh or ankle as they ate on the run. I put some feed closer to me. The piglets were starting to get used to my smell and presence. They came closer and didn't dart away. They let me touch them as I emptied more of the feed onto the floor. They all had the same shape of ear; it was a teardrop, a longer, droopier ear than others I'd seen, but not so much that it covered their line of vision.

Soon the little pigs allowed me to pet them without any protest. I picked one up. He squirmed and tried to right his body to leap from my arms, but once he smelled the molasses on my hand he fell in love with me. He nibbled on my left hand, licking as much of my skin as he could, breathing quickly, making soft little grunts as he searched for more. His hair was soft as corn silk; it was shiny and faint, as if the colors did not originate from the hair at all, but rather were inked onto the skin by some magical treatment their mother deployed as they left her womb, like a factory, I thought.

The piglet in my arms got lots of pellets. The others scurried around and wouldn't let me give them the special treatment. Before long the burlap bag was empty and the litter began to stroll back to the red cone of light, flopping their tiny bodies down under the heat and falling asleep with full tummies. I looked down at the baby pig held awkwardly in the bend of my elbow. His eyes were closed, thick lashes shut, his small head easing up and down as he breathed. He was warm, but I pulled the empty burlap bag over him anyway. I hadn't been paying attention to what Derrick and Darren were doing since I'd gotten into the pen, but now I could hear all the sounds of the farrowing house as I let my head rest on the partition behind me.

There was a dull hum coming off all the heating lamps, and in the distance, as if I were listening through a can on a string, I heard light squeals. I didn't want to think about what was happening, knowing full well that the tail docking was going down. Instead, I let myself drift into a napping state like the baby I held. I thought of my mother and wondered if she was going to die. I allowed myself to dream about being president like Jimmy, telling voters on the campaign trail the awful story of how my mother had been a hard-working woman but died early. As I drifted off, I imagined that dreams were possible. I'd finally gotten into the birthing house. If I could do that, then surely people would vote for a man with awful-looking fingers.

Break-Fist at Noon

10

The table was full of good-smelling foods, steam rising as if the bowls and plates were on fire; the aromas of flour and egg fried in oil clung to the thick air in the kitchen. Our sisters had made more than my mother would've ever permitted. Pancakes were stacked nearly a foot high on a crystal platter my mother only used for taking food to an elderly person we didn't know very well. A bowl of homemade syrup sat bubbling next to two plates of blackened bacon and sausage. Dana, hardly able to lift a pancake from the pile, told us she was going to pray for the food. "I want you to put your heads down like at church in Terre Haute."

She clasped her tiny floury hands together and prayed. "The God in heaven make our break-fist good. And please God in heaven get Mommy home now."

She looked up with a painful grin on her sticky face and clapped loudly for herself. Darren spoke up. "Good job." He pointed toward the corner where a plank of maple wood leaned against the wall. "Let's put the other leaf in the table."

Derrick and Darren picked up the leaf and placed it respectfully against the stove, and like moving men took hold of each end of the table and expertly eased it open, careful not to spill a drop of the syrup or the milk in our glasses. They slid the leaf into place and gently closed the gap until the table was one again, long and spacious. We all sat back down and reveled in the added leaf. It was like a ceremony had been performed. Our mother only put the extra leaf in on the rare occasions we'd have company. Now, with the food before us like the Last Supper portrait on the wall at our grandparents' house, the meal seemed spiritual.

We dug in and ate quickly. Derrick cut my pancakes for me while Dina kept getting up from the table to bring more butter or knives or forks. It was nearly noontime, and we'd been up since our mother had been driven away by our dad. We were all tired. My brothers had let me sleep in the pen with the baby pigs until it was time to bring the sows back in. The baby pig had escaped my arms while I slept. When Darren woke me up and helped me out of the crate, he told me to not look down at the floor, to keep right on walking until I got to the other end of the building and went outside.

I was partially asleep and stumbled down the aisle toward the door. I started to remember what he said and looked down anyway. At my feet were hundreds of little tails of every color. They stuck to the wet concrete like snipped-off hair curls or some kind of weird worms. I could feel them squish under my boots as I picked up the pace. I'd done well not to get upset and wanted to get out before I blew it. By the time I reached the door and yanked it open, I was trembling. A bright wedge of outdoor light slanted onto the floor. I jumped over the door frame and struggled to pull the heavy door shut again. Outside, by myself, I walked around with my head down, sniffling and talking to myself, asking questions I didn't know the answers to. Cut-off fingers, cut-off tails, a bleeding mother; it was all too much to make sense of.

But now, with food galore, I wasn't thinking about much more than how good breakfast for lunch tasted. I knew where bacon and sausage came from and steered away from the thought. I ate big bites of pancake and drank two mason jars full of milk. It was a fantastic time for us. Work had acted as an ice pack on our worried hearts. Soon we began to giggle and then laugh out loud, open mouths full of food, giddy with the realization that we were free to act as goofy as we wanted.

Derrick tossed a pancake onto the center of the table; it made a funny noise as it hit the Formica top. Darren said, "Now that's what I call a flapjack slap!" We burst into more laughter, Dana laughing just because everyone else was. Milk came out of her red nose. She covered her face and tried to get control, but the damage had been done. Her laugh turned to a small sob, then developed into a full-fledged bawl. Dina tried to comfort her, telling her it was OK, not to be embarrassed. We put our forks down and tried to comfort her, too. She was able to talk after wiping her mouth and nose with a dishtowel. With her eyes wet, lashes gluey, she asked, "Is Mommy going to come back?"

"Yes," Darren said, his head bowed, flicking a piece of sausage around his plate with the tip of his fork. The uncertainty in his voice caused us all to spiral down from our earlier flightiness. Before long we all had our heads down as if we were praying at the end of the meal, crying as a group, as a unit of brothers and sisters who hadn't ever before considered our lives without our parents. There was silence for a long time. Dina and Dana held hands; I'd gone to sit on Darren's lap. Derrick kept to himself, blowing his nose into another dishtowel. The phone rang. Derrick jumped up from the table and ran to answer it. He came back just as quickly as he'd gone.

"That was Dad. Mom is in the recovery room. He said she's going to be fine. She can come home in two days. He told us to make sure to get the evening chores done 'cause he won't be home until after dark." Dana started clapping once again. Darren stood, hiking up his pants by the belt loops, a gesture I told myself to remember to try later. He said, "Let's get back to work then." I stood up too, wishing I had on pants that had loops, not the elastic band at my chubby waist, like a baby. The girls began ridding the table of our leftovers, scraping what was salvageable onto one plate, the scraps into a bowl for Joe and the boars.

As we were pulling on our boots, another shot rang out. It made us all jump and propelled us to the living room window in a flash, rumbling through the house, its weak foundation giving under our feet. At the large window, we crowded ourselves into a jam. We looked around the yard and the edges of the field. Nothing. Craning our necks, we searched in every direction until Darren shouted, "There!" Out of the dark green cornfield, a fast moving shank of fur shot into the gravel lane. As it slowed, we could name it. "Joe, boy!" Dana said with glee, pointing. He trotted up the lane toward the house, his ears perked as if nothing had happened, a pink swish of tongue lolling over his muzzle. When another shot blasted into the air from our neighbor's farm to warn Joe to not come back, Darren shook his head and motioned us all away from the window. Joe acted as if nothing had happened; he had a smile on his face. Derrick spoke. "Come on," he said. "That dumb dog is going to get killed one of these days." Dana shot back, pouty, "Joe's not dumb!"

"Oh yeah, then why doesn't he come when you call his name?" said Derrick. He walked out, leaving us in the center of the room, watching Joe through the window as he dug cool dirt from under a tree and rubbed his head in the divot, particularly his ears, as if he were trying to soothe them. "He's not dumb," Dana repeated. "He's just bad sometimes."

It's Home and It's Weird

11

My mother's hysterectomy was complete. She stayed in the hospital for a couple more days and then came home looking weary, dark circles under her eyes, her normally poofy hair smooshed down, bangs flat and oily on her forehead. It was late afternoon when my father drove her up to the porch in the station wagon. The five of us stood on the steps, waiting anxiously for her to come into the house. We'd worked hard to make it nice. The girls had made another breakfast-dinner, and Derrick and Darren had washed two big loads of laundry while I swept the floor in the living room, the broom clumsy in my left hand. We'd cut fresh rhubarb, and put white and yellow flock in a Mrs. Butterworth bottle on the center of the table, a lilac branch stuck in the middle, a purple ball hovering above the more common weeds.

My dad flopped out of the car and scurried to help my mother. She clutched her purse under her arm and held a basket from the hospital that contained a small plastic pitcher-cup set in her hand; it was an ugly, dull mustard color. She walked slowly toward us, her smile sort of creepy, fixed and empty, as if she didn't know who we were and was merely making eye contact to be polite. I knew what had happened to her had to do with her private parts, that she'd never have another baby and that I wasn't supposed to mention anything about it or to say anything about how Darren and Derrick had let me in on what went wrong. At night, in bed, whispering, Derrick had said, "Mom had her tubes tied 'cause they exploded." I pictured copper plumbing up inside her, wondering how it got there and why it had broken. I was relieved she'd not had a lobotomy, although her mind did seem altered, perhaps rearranged. Darren had also lectured us all on what it meant.

Around the kitchen table, just minutes before our parents were to arrive from the hospital, he'd said, "Now, remember, don't bring up the hospital. It costs a lot and they are not going to want to talk about it." He looked directly at me to assure me nothing was my fault. "With Dougie's hand and Mom getting sick, the bills are going to be big. Just hug her and stuff when they get home." His reassurance hadn't helped. I felt like I'd let them down, that it was my fault we were not going to have enough money for the down payment on a farm, or worse, not enough to feed and clothe us.

Our mother carried her hospital goodies as if they were a bundle of roses. At the steps, she formally presented her cheek for kissing. She'd never done that in the past. Now, with her face tilted, temple, ear, and cheek slanted at just the right angle for us to kiss, I thought they'd taken her brain out of her head any- way. Maybe, I pondered, her plumbing started at the top and twisted and turned down through her body; there'd been a kink in the midsection that caused a backup and POW! I'd seen a water hose act the same way in the barn lot. It was just how things declined over time. Shears broke, cupolas cracked, beams splintered, and plumbing burst. All items on the farm needed constant replacing. It was costly and frustrating; just when you thought you'd caught up and were on the path to a better place, something broke that you hadn't expected and the cycle of worry and regret began all over again.

Derrick and Darren kissed my mother and told her how good she looked, even though their faces showed what they were thinking. They had expressions that said, "Who is this person with wild eyes posing as our mother, acting if she were the Queen of England sashaying up the steps to her castle?"

I kissed my mother as she paused in front of each of us, bending at the knees ever so daintily for a peck, getting some sugar from her adoring subjects. She made a kissing sound herself when she got to Dina and asked, "A smooch-kiss, please." My mother had to stoop down in front of Dana to get a loud smacker planted right on her nose. Our little sister looked at her and wrinkled her narrow brow. "You look funny, Mommy. Stop that!" she said with a giggle, as if she'd caught her in a silly game. My mother ignored her and brushed by us into the house. We followed her, freaked out by her new demeanor, yet intrigued by it as well.

My mother surveyed the house and spotted the lilac centerpiece. She became emotional. Crying, with her hand over her heart she said, "Oh, my goodness. You children are just perfect." In an instant, her face changed, going from teary-eyed to straight-faced in a flash. Something just under her skin seemed to break and collapse inward. She became perturbed, eyes chatoyant and turning to lasers of green, like an evil comic-book character. "I just hope none of you have to have what I had done. It hurt. It still does."

She switched back again, her breath coming in scallops, sputtering as she talked. "I am so sorry," she cried. "I am not a woman anymore."

She sat down at the kitchen table and put her head in her hands. Our dad seemed stuck in neutral; he neither stepped forward nor turned to leave, he just watched my mother along with the rest of us. We stared at her, trying to determine if the hospital had switched mothers at discharge, or if somehow they'd implanted a chip in her brain, one that told her to behave like an aging movie star whose time had passed. We watched her there at the table for a while, the sunlight pouring in through the kitchen window, frosting the flowers on the table in chrome and touching her hair so that it appeared to be truly graying. Finally, our dad walked to her side and took her by the arm. "Doris, let's get you into bed. Doctor said two days in bed and then you can begin taking walks."

He led her out of the room, leaving the five of us more than puzzled. I remember thinking about a game we always wanted, Operation, where you try and remove a body part with a pair of tweezers without the patient's red nose lighting up. The room was silent until Dana spoke. "She's so silly." She ran to Derrick to be picked up. We all went outside to the porch and sat down. It was beautiful; the sky was so blue it hurt to look at, and the corn rose up tall beside the lane where ditch mallow bloomed in pink and rose along the hummocks like icing on a wedding cake. Inside we could hear our mother sobbing, again telling our father she was sorry. Was it true what she'd said? That she wasn't a woman anymore? Could it be that she'd undergone a surgery that made her not a woman? And if that were true, was she still our mother?

I didn't ask these questions as we sat in silence. Before long, each of us picked up a shank of limestone from the driveway to write on the concrete porch. Darren started it. He drew a large heart, our mother's initials in the center, and the words, "GET WELL SOON!" written in perfect block letters to the side where the arrow tip shot right through the middle. We all worked at our own special drawings on separate sections of the cement. When we were done, there were smiley faces and balloons, smaller hearts swarming around the larger one Darren had drawn, and Dina had written in her best cursive the initials *T.I.D.* and *T.I.N.D.,* true-if-destroyed, true-if-not-destroyed, a perfect promise for our message to become reality whether the wind and rain took it away or if it simply remained there forever, preserved. Either way, we stood up and stretched our backs, once again soothed by the faithful need of chores to be done.

Devil Worshippers

12

For days, we kids were left to carry the burden of the farm and home. Our father did his best to care for our mother, taking her cold glasses of water and loaves of toast with honey on a TV tray. I don't think he ate anything during those days, not with us, anyway. As we brushed ourselves off on the porch or ate together at the kitchen table, we could hear our mother bawling and then chattering nonstop for hours on end, our dad apparently listening to it all behind the door of their bedroom. His parents were due back any day, and it showed in the tiny glimpses we'd get of him as he walked briskly to the bathroom for tissue or carried the food from kitchen to bed. His eyes looked as strange as our mother's had on the day she came home. He looked thinner, and for the first time I noticed he had some gray in his hair. Had it turned that way overnight? Was he so worried about our mother's plumbing, the medical bills, and what his parents would think when they came home to find I'd lost fingers and their daughter-in-law was no longer a woman, that the hair tried to show it? I didn't know. I couldn't decide if anyone else knew either, least of all him. He threw himself whole-heartedly into caring for his wife, and it was taking a toll on him.

The days wore on, slowly. My fingers still needed soaking twice a day: saltwater pain in the morning and at night, bookends for the hours in between. It was not pleasant, but I was helped along by my brothers and sisters, all of whom took turns (except Dana, who got to act like she was my nurse at every soak) cutting off the bandages and preparing the water. Darren enticed me to deal with the situation by promising more visits to the farrowing house, where the baby pigs seemed to multiply exponentially.

One morning, Darren and Derrick had let me sleep in and hadn't shaken me awake for the morning chores. The accident had left me without a routine and time off from the normal farmwork. While my grandpa had strict rules about the age when a boy could handle the farrowing house, we'd always been expected to do our fair share. Now, however, with my hand nearly useless, my feelings were hurt not to have been woken up to watch the chores being performed from afar, a safe distance away from any potential infectors.

I got up and looked out the window. Outside the tulip tree leaves blew in the breeze, their yellow flowers diving to the ground below, making the grass underneath appear to be littered with cracked teacups. I pulled on my overalls and shot down the stairs. To my surprise our mother sat at the kitchen table, Dana on her lap, reading *Ranger Rick*. Dana, who'd just turned six, said nonchalantly, "Look, Dougie, Mommy came out." My mother turned and looked at me standing in the doorway. The skin under her eyes was now fully black, and her face was as white as paper. The combination made her look like a raccoon. She didn't speak, only motioned for me to come to her. Dana was busy drawing, while Dina made biscuits at the counter, flour puffing into the air as she threw the dough down, punching the center with a tight fist coated in dusty white. She was thirteen, and in many ways had started to mother the rest of us.

"Where're Dad and the other boys?" I asked. My mother didn't answer. She'd turned back to reading to Dana, her voice so low I couldn't tell if she was reading what was in the magazine or something she'd made up or recited from memory, like the stuff she whispered in my ear. Dina didn't turn from the biscuits, but answered me.

"They're out with the sows. Dad told us to keep you in here. He doesn't want your fingers getting infected." I was mad. I'd gotten to know some of the baby pigs by heart and was able to distinguish nearly identical ones by referring to my diary. A speck on a left ear, the angle of a snout, the size of a tail nub told me who was who. I made sure to record the details of some of the pigs, noting which crate they lived in and which sow was their mother. I'd felt like I'd gotten a good start on what was going to be the work of my handicapped summer. I'd know so much about the year's piglet crop that my grandfather would have to respect me as a hog man. It would be a story I'd tell on the campaign trail with Darren. Red, white, and blue buttons with our faces in a pig outline: Vote for the Crandell Boys! But that seemed to be coming to a halt as my father had ordered me to stay away. I kicked the floor in the kitchen. My mother was unaware of my discontent. She stopped reading to hold Dana's arm oddly as she drew a picture, as if my mother's hold prevented her from falling off a cliff, not simply steadying her little hand to make the correct line on the paper. I walked to the pantry and got two empty bread bags.

I went out the door and walked to the edge of the barn lot. I could navigate the pasture's trails and make it to the farrowing house undetected. The house my grandparents occupied was on the same farm, owned by Grady, just across the scary pasture. My grandfather in an act of total meanness made certain all the baby pigs were born on his side of the cash-rented farm. I thought little of him for it. I took a step forward into the deep, grassy thicket. I didn't want to cross the pasture alone, but if I showed up ready to work, willing to get on with it and round up pigs for medicine, ignoring the docked tails, brave enough to inflict the necessary pain of care, my father would have to let me in. He'd just have to.

I was scared to walk through the pasture alone. Our cash-rented farm was near an area of the county that was rumored to have a secret lair of devil worshippers. Everyone knew that they lived in the flat plains just a mile or so down the road in a place called The Prairie. Most of them stayed in three enormous houses, set back on long lanes, the outsheds sealed up with boards and the fields in front gone to pot. Year after year high schoolers rode out there in pickup trucks, armed with sticks and garlic strands, their coats zipped up tightly, hands in gloves, not mittens; if it came to the worst and you needed to fight off a devil worshipper, you had to have your fingers free. One story was the most grue-some. A man from Schwanns, the ice cream and frozen foods delivery business that used to roam the roads of most rural areas, came up missing after he'd been last seen driving in the lane of one of the devil farms to ask for directions. The story goes that he knocked on the door and an old woman answered, her hair as black as death, the wrinkles on her face over two hundred years old. She invited the deliveryman inside and told him to sit down while she got her son to explain the directions. She told the visitor that she was an old woman and couldn't remember her middle name, let alone north and south, east and west.

The deliveryman sat at the red table looking around the kitchen, noticing how the room throbbed, as if he were inside a heart. The walls were maroon, the counters black, and the ceiling had no lights, yet it was very bright sitting at the table, his clipboard in hand, sharpened pencil ready to note the directions back to Wabash.

The old woman returned with a man who appeared to be blind. His eyes were milky and nearly shut, yet he didn't seem to need any help walking. The son approached the table and sat down very close to the deliveryman. He started giving the directions but his speech was too clipped and rushed for the deliveryman to write anything down. The son started chanting the directions, which sent the deliveryman off his seat and ready to head for the door. But the son grabbed him and fully opened his eyes, which were catlike and rose-colored, yellow pupils throbbing like the room, as he spoke in tongues. The old woman began to wheeze and cackle, a knife in her hand. The last thing the deliveryman saw was the mother and son above him, holding his body to the sticky floor with uncommon strength, their eyes wild, the bleating noise of a goat escaping from their juicy mouths.

Two days later the refrigerated truck was found just inside the city limits, driven there by a man, a witness reported, who appeared blind, but it was hard to tell, the bystander said, the suspect disappeared before she could get a real good look. Inside the truck, the remains of what appeared to be a butchered hog were found, meat dangling from bones nicked with a cleaver. It was an odd find, the police said, but it could've been someone had used the refrigerated truck to keep a hog carcass cool until they removed all the meat. That is, before the officers looked up front in the driver's seat, where the deliveryman's head sat neatly on a hand towel, this note stuck into his forehead with a thumbtack: "Don't ask for directions when you go to HELL!"

It was a terrifying story, one that on some level I knew of course was not true, but I couldn't keep from nipping at my fear whenever I had to run from our house to our grandparents', through the pasture that boasted a towering overgrowth of ragweed and thistle, some of it so tall it could've been mistaken for trees. I picked up the pace and began to run along the path. Birds exploded from the weeds, causing me to tighten every muscle, my chubby buns clenched until they ached. I thought I heard an old woman's voice behind me. I ran as hard as I could, my bread bags whipping in the air, the smell of mown alfalfa shifting to a burning, acrid fume. I was breathing heavily, trying to make it through the last few bends of the narrow trail, when I fell over a log in the path, my hurt hand under me. I didn't spend a second on the dusty ground; I shot straight up and sprinted the rest of the way, no pain in me whatsoever until I got to the farrowing house.

The mound of gauze on my hand had blood on it, and for a moment I thought the old woman and her hellhound son had actually accosted me out in the pasture. I was scared but focused. I knew if my fingers tattled on me, if my father spotted the blood, I was doomed. Quickly, I placed the bags over my hand, making certain the lettering covered the bloody spot on the gauze. I tucked the ends of the bags into the bottom of the gauze and put on the toughest man's face I could muster. I knocked on the door. No one came. I kicked on the boards at the base. My dad came to the door, slid it open, stepped out, and closed it again.

"What is it, son? Is your mother OK?" He was sweaty, the wide sideburns on his jaws dripping. I shook my head no. I said, trying to sound official, "No, sir. I am here to work."

He shook his head no before I could even go on with my manly speech. "Not today, Dougie," he said. He looked as if he were trying to complete a complex cipher in his head, his eyes slightly crossed, lips pursed, trying to speak. Finally he said, winded, "Your grandpa is going to be back in a few days. You know how he feels about you kids being in here before you're ready. I shouldn't have let you come in with your brothers anyway." He rubbed my head and went back inside. I'd been hiding my hand behind my back, and when I pulled it back, I could see the spot on the gauze had gotten bigger. Trickles of blood had smeared on the inside of the bags. I didn't care. I tried to think of what to do next. I could knock again and risk angering my dad or I could sneak in, which would result in the same. I decided to look around the back of the birthing house to see if I could find a way inside.

I held my hand up, hoping the blood would somehow seep back into me. My fingers stung, and the one most damaged felt loose, like it had come off and was swimming in the bag like a goldfish. I'd been having phantom sensations for days but didn't know what to call them. I just assumed it was part of having something on your body ripped free. As I sidestepped the brooks of liquid manure moving slowly downhill, oozing from underneath the building, I wondered if my mother's lady parts felt the way my fingers did, there and not there at the same time. It was too much to think about for very long, so I concentrated on finding a gap in the boards or a knothole to peek through.

I spotted a small hinged panel near the end of the building. I became excited thinking I'd found a way to at least watch the piglets. I tromped through the manure; something crunched under my feet as I moved through the gooey mass. I stopped and looked down. I was standing ankle deep in afterbirth. There were purple strands and knotty red cords, white masses of clear sacs. Wetness oozed over the ends of my boots. I gagged. I knew what came out of a sow when she had babies, but the afterbirths of twenty sows was something I was not prepared to see. I pulled my feet free as though it were quicksand. I heard the sounds of cracking under my feet again. When I was out of the mess, I looked back at my footprints as they slowly filled with the goo. I saw several fetal pigs, stillborn, stuck in the manure, their little eyes shut, lips parted ever so slightly, and their tails long, not docked. It shocked me. I also knew that things died on the farm, sometimes before they ever got started, but the babies with full tails sent me as quick as I could trudge to the opening on the building. More now than ever, I needed to see live romping piglets scurrying around the pens, soft and real and clean.

The panel door was just the right height. It locked from the outside. I quietly slid the butterfly lock to open it. I looked in cautiously. A good view of three litters of pigs came into focus. There were over thirty baby pigs playing in a large group, new ones, apparently born the day before, all up and eager to get silly in chase while their mammoth mothers were out. I felt better just watching them. I could hear my dad giving Derrick and Darren instructions about which litter to work on next, but I couldn't see them. I watched the minuscule herd as they pretended to be full grown, scratching their tiny hips on a wood plank as if they'd been doing it for years. When I was five I'd gotten to weigh a newborn piglet at the county fair as part of a guessing game in the midway. The idea was that the carnie would give anyone who could guess the weight of a piglet a stuffed pink or blue pig if they could guess the weight within an ounce. We did a lot to baby pigs when they were born, but we never weighed them. No pig farmer we knew did. So the game was difficult, even for pig boys. I didn't get it right. I was off by almost ten ounces. The baby I'd chosen weighed two pounds nine ounces.

The piglets played and ran around in the pen, oinking and acting like little fools. I noticed a very small piglet in the corner. He was hard to see. He didn't move with the others and didn't look very happy. A regular-sized piglet nuzzled the tiny piglet until it came into the light of the pen. He was a runt. I'd heard of such piglets but had never seen one. He was so small he could've fit easily into my hand. His hair was fuzzy and he was black on both ends, belted in the center by a slim band of white. He hung his tiny head low. The rest of the babies had their tails docked, but his was not. It was so small it looked like a Cheerio. I smiled as I watched him. I wanted to crawl through the opening and feed him some good vitamin pellets to help him catch up with the others. Another piglet rushed by him, snapping playfully at the little thing but knocking him over on his side in the process. The runt strained to right himself, wobbling on the floor until he got enough motion to stand back up. His short legs trembled as he stood in a cone of light, trying to regain his bearings. I had to get in there, I thought. He needs me. I opened the panel further and picked up a board from the soggy ground to wedge it so I could determine if my plump body would fit through the hole. The runt shivered, his little head lower, as the rest of the litter leaped and scurried around. He was all alone in the middle of a big, fat family; he was there but not there, he was my mother's body, my hand—incomplete, marred, and wholly different.

My boots slipped on the boards under the opening as I pawed with the tips of my feet to gain footing to pull myself inside the farrowing house. I tried again and again, but my heavy bottom and stocky legs wouldn't allow me to get through. I thought of getting a good run at the opening, stepping back and rushing at it full speed, leaping through the space, somersaulting into the pigpen, snatching the runt into my arms, and fighting off my brothers and father as they tried to wrest the piglet from my clutches. But I knew my body wouldn't cooperate. Instead, I tried to entice the little runt to me by using the power of my mind. I concentrated on him, fixed my gaze on his nominal head, the noggin that looked downy, like a baby bird, the center a soft ridge of fur like a tiny mohawk. He moved forward ever so slightly; I honed in more on the mindmeld. I repeated in my head: "Come here, come here, come here." Once again the swarm of other piglets knocked him down. They scrambled to nibble on the feed pouring into the trough. I ducked so whoever was doing the feeding wouldn't see me. I peeked over the bottom of the opening. My father stood watching the piglets. I could only see the top half of him, his round face and bushy sideburns, the flannel shirt, T-shirt underneath, even though it was hot out. Dark hair sprouted from his collar as if it were responding to the warmth, trying to bloom. He scratched his chin and bent down to inspect the runt pig. He picked him up. I was jealous. My dad held the little pig in front of his face, so close I imagined he could feel the hot breath from the runt's nostrils. My dad talked to the runt quietly, whispering and producing a sound he usually made to our little sister. I felt better for the runt. I hoped my father wasn't going to dock his tail or give him a shot that hurt, unless the medicine would make him sturdier, less vulnerable to his siblings.

I strained to watch while giving extra effort to not being detected. I slumped down more and made sure not to breathe too loudly. My hand hurt. I glanced down at it quickly, not wanting to miss what was happening. The bread bags felt heavier, slushy. I saw that the bag held a considerable pool of blood. It swished when I moved the bags for a better view. More blood dripped from the gauze, filling the bags more and more with each drop. I told myself to worry about that later; for now I had a runt to watch over.

I made my eyes get accustomed to looking inside again. I couldn't see the runt or my father until the edges of murk began to recede and it all cleared up, a TV warming into focus. My dad had put the runt on a board. The tiny thing lay on his side as if he'd decided to take a nap. I knew I had to make myself watch the shot or tail docking; if I was ever going to be a real farmer, I had to be able to do what was best. The runt didn't move as my dad continued cooing. The little pig cried a little squeal, light and quick, a sound that said he was ready. My dad's hand rose just above the runt's head; the ball-peen hammer he held seemed to hover on its own. What did he need it for? Was part of the crate broken? Was the runt being shown the hammer? Did he need to see it for some reason?

I blinked my eyes. The hammer fell like a light switch had been turned off and on again quickly. A tiny pop made my stomach hurt. The runt didn't move. He lay on the small board, his downy hair lightly blowing. My father stroked his small body, talking to him. I finally understood what had happened and gasped loudly, a noise I hadn't planned; it made my father look up from the runt. Our eyes locked. He shook his head, hung it for a second, and then looked back up at me. "Dougie!" he yelled.

I turned to run, sloshing back through the afterbirth swamp. I strained to lug myself over the awful terrain. I took one last, heavy stride to get it over with. My boots tripped me up. I fell on the outermost rim of the muck, my hand once again under my pudgy waist as I went splat, face down. I struggled up, the bread bags now fallen off, my gauzy hand brown and heavy, sopping with liquid. My brothers shot around the corner of the building, my father behind, telling them to get me, shouting to have them bring me to the water spigot to wash off. I tried to evade them, to fake them out and run in another direction, but it was no good. Darren got ahold of me and pulled me to him. He didn't say a word as he tried to keep me from fighting him. Derrick jerked a hose from the side of the building, water gushing out full force, clear and cold. I gave up and let them pull the soiled bandages from my hand. My dad took me from Darren and bent down to aim the water on my fingers more precisely. He told Derrick to turn it down. The water trickled over my fingers, as much blood now coming out as water. My dad held my horrible fingers in his hand when it was over. He told me we had to get to the house to wash them in the antiseptic. I couldn't catch my breath. I hated him and loved him all at once. When he picked me up, slumped over his shoulder, he was talking to me softly, the same sound he made for the runt just before he did what was best.

Third-Person Mother Cometh

13

It was so hot the second week of June in 1976 that we had to put a box fan in each crate in the farrowing house to keep the sows cooled off. It was a difficult prospect. The baby pigs still needed the heat from the warming lamps for a least a week after they were born; yet their mothers were sweltering as they did their best to nurse the babies without getting overheated. To make it worse, a sow grunts when she lies on her side to attract the piglets to suckle; all the grunting requires heavy breathing, which then causes even more overheating. The sows were constantly on guard, using all their senses to protect their offspring, and I couldn't help but wonder if my mother had somehow lost what they had in such abundance.

I hadn't talked with my father since the incident with the runt. He seemed content with me coming to my own terms with what I'd witnessed. For my part, I remained solemn and withdrawn, even ignoring Darren when the issue came up. He was working on a hose on the porch when I walked out the door and headed to the pasture, not saying a word to him as I passed.

"Doug, come here and help me with this," he said, pointing to the length of green hose he had wrapped over his shoulder, some of it falling down as he pulled a pocketknife from a leather case at his waist. I stopped but didn't turn toward him.

"Come on," he said, "you can help me punch holes in it. We have to put this in with the boars to keep them cool."

I turned around and walked back to him. He handed me an ice pick and told me to be careful. "Sit down and use it on the porch." While he cut tiny slits in the hose, he also watched to make sure I was not going to jab the ice pick into my leg. I pushed the sharp tip into the nylon hose until I could feel it scratch the cement underneath. The idea was to create a watering tube that would seep enough over the hot day's hours to allow the boars to wallow in fresh water but not be wasteful or make a muddy area in the pen that could cause flies to come and give birth.

We performed the task in silence. I could feel him looking at me, trying to figure out if talking to me again about the realities of farming would do any good. The small slices his blade made in the tough hose squeaked like in a cartoon. He exaggerated the sound, wiggling the blade to create a more rapid squeak. I tried to keep a smile from creasing my face. He squeaked more until I finally cracked up. Then I got mad again.

"You know, I could round up all the runts and you could raise them yourself." He went back to making regular cuts on the hose. I put the ice pick down and tried not to appear too excited. I watched him as he allowed more of the hose to fall to the porch, each loop building on the next, a stack of it up to his knee.

"Would I get to feed them and give them baths?"

"That all depends. You're gonna have to know that once they get big enough to sell, you can't act like a baby and all." He cut the end of the hose off and shoved a large cork into it, making it look like a boa had swallowed some prey.

"OK," I said. He looked at me with a crinkle between his eyes. He raised his brows as a sign I needed to convince him some more. "I...I know they have to be sold and stuff." He licked his lips; a split was continually in the center of his bottom one, like a prizefighter who didn't allow enough time between bouts to heal right. I wanted my lip to look that way too, even going as far as pulling it from the sides to get it to pop open. I wondered how we were going to look on our Vote for Us! posters with bottom lips like that. I decided it would be part of our appeal; after all, lots of farmers had lips like those. It would be like Jimmy holding up peanuts; it would be our trademark, that and my healed-up, perfectly normal fingers, and a herd of my runt pigs in the background. All of us alive and well, that's how I saw it right then. I couldn't have predicted how much could fall apart in such a short time. No, right then, with Darren telling me I could save all the runt pigs on the farm, I felt I could heal them all, and my mother, and my fingers as well. I could do it. I'd have to try.

My mother came out of the house and stood on the porch watching us. She looked tired and wild with energy all at once, her face like a mask, tight and strained, about to break apart at any moment. She stared at Darren and me for some time before she finally said, "Dougie, get in here." She pointed toward the house. "Your mother wants you to soak your fingers. She needs to look at them. She's worried about you." It was the first time I heard her talk in the third person. It was scary. I'd get used to it, we all would, but now it sounded as creepy as a mummy's voice in some black-and-white horror movie.

I got up reluctantly and walked to the screen door she held open. Before I went into the house for the Epsom soak, I made eye contact with my brother. With no words at all, he promised me everything would be fine, if I'd just keep making it better. Day by day.

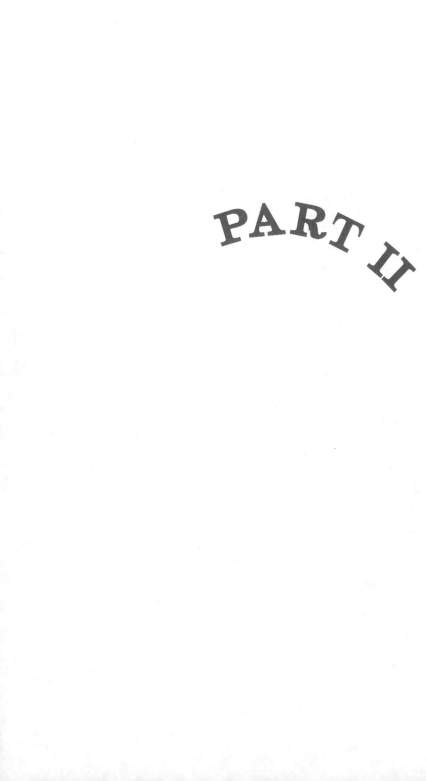

PART II

Peanut and Other Other Runts

14

The plan we came up with was simple: Darren would arrive early at the farrowing house each morning before my dad and would survey all the new arrivals for baby pigs that would be considered runty or otherwise too disabled to be allowed to live. He'd pluck the little guys from underneath the heating lamps and place them gingerly into a gunnysack for me to retrieve just before breakfast.

On the first morning of our covert piglet rescue, Darren snuck quietly into the kitchen from the back porch, through a door we were never to use because it opened up onto a mossy, dank area that smelled of wet earth. A trickle of water could be heard under a piece of rotting plywood that covered a hole that fell straight toward hell. We were made to believe that death itself was housed right underneath that bowed piece of wood our landlord had slapped down. He had spray-painted the words: Stay Off!! It was actually an open cistern that our parents warned us could swallow us up and drag us down to China. They made us believe we would be held captive inside a gigantic and rancid whale's belly. "Think of Jonah," our mother would say. "He just barely got out, and that took God's help." We didn't know what she was talking about, of course, because we didn't go to Sunday school, but she'd attended it throughout her childhood. We thought her warning was just another aspect of having had her womanly area altered for good.

From the secret door, Darren peeked in at me sitting at the kitchen table with my bundled hand rested on top of an over-turned and perpetually empty bread box. Our family required so much bread in a week that we simply piled the bags of sliced bread on the counter, rather than stowing it away in the tin antique rectangle with perforated swirls of half-moons that my arm rested on.

He whispered to me, "Hey, come here." Something strained his shoulder down as he held it outside the door. I got up quietly and looked around, made sure my mother was still asleep and the girls busy in the living room dusting. As I walked past the open window of the kitchen I could smell the hot July sun baking the silk on the ears of corn in the two-hundred-acre field directly behind the house. A garish electric clock the shape of a bronze teapot clicked off seconds as I made my way toward him. The house that wasn't ours creaked as I walked, made little groans beneath the floorboards that reminded me of how Joe would whimper and arch his back when I rubbed his ears. Darren was smiling, and as I got closer I could tell that what he held in a gunnysack squirmed at the end of his arm, making his taut bicep flex into an oval just below the short sleeve of his white T-shirt.

Darren pointed to my gumboots, a signal to come with him. I slid my feet into the floppy boots and stepped out the back door. I followed him around the plywood that he sometimes would tease me contained a lion pit with huge bamboo stakes, just like in Chuck Norris movies. We cut a wide berth around the cistern and headed toward one of the many old sheds that we never used. The main barn was an impressive, towering, red, boxy building with a milk house at one end and at the other a defunct silo and a concrete feeding lot that could hold up to two hundred shoats for fattening at self-feeders. The main barn was painted every year by our landlord's help. They never failed to use bright white paint to stencil in huge block lettering the name GRADY at the highest point of the façade, just below the towering weather vanes and the rooster-adorned cupola. The rest of the outbuildings either sheltered old farm implements from the failed cash renters before us or were simply vacant and dusty, exhilarating cubbies to hole up in during a high-octane round of hide-and-seek. I peed my pants once in one of those dusty corners when I hid so well even I couldn't find the way out.

The shed we walked into was an old-timey grain bin with four wooden compartments that ran up to the ceiling and formed a high rectangle, and a hallway that I could tell had recently been swept; the broom's marks were etched into the ancient dust that still clung to the cracked cement. The building was the furthest back from the house, well hidden with weeds growing up around the foundation. Fescue and wild rye shot up over our heads and hid the building up to its middle.

Once inside the shed, near the back, where I now noticed two fresh bales of straw, a bag of filched piglet feed, and a little plastic shovel, Darren set the bag down and looked at me like we did at Christmastime; we'd learned it was the opening, the anticipation of the gift, not what was inside that made us feel good. He motioned for me to come closer and I did, my oversized boots flapping like a seal. He bent down and pulled a piece of jute from around the secured top of the gunny, eased down the bag to expose six little oddly colored, fuzzy, and variously shaped runt pigs. In the dark it was hard to see them completely until Darren pulled on a long string above his head. A bulb shone down on the baby pigs as if angels were descending.

Three of the runts were all white, two all black, and one, the littlest and nearest death, was a gray piglet, small as a hamster. It was a girl piglet. She shook all over, scared from being trapped inside the sack. I fell on my knees and began to brush the little things softly on their hunched backs. Darren had done it. He'd gone like the Christ we'd heard about from our mother's parents and saved the blind, the leper, and the feeble from the farrowing house, rescued them from the very grip of what I'd been told was a painless death, as if that would comfort a pig boy.

I knelt for only an instant before Darren got down to serious business. He had to get me in line before I blew it all by getting too excited and ruining the entire scheme.

"OK, listen, Doug." It was the first time I can recall that he called me Doug and not Dougie.

"I've rigged up the light here." He pointed to the string that dangled before his tanned face. There'd been no electricity to the building, something that was common on lots of the farms in that area. The first electrically lighted city in the world had farms on the outskirts of town at the end of the 1970s that still didn't have power; later I'd understand the irony.

He pulled a dreaded Wonder Bread bag from his front pocket. I'd spied the colorful fringe of it earlier and had hoped he'd forget about it and not make me pull it over my hand. The Wonder Bread bags went on and on that summer. It felt like I was bagging up something dead, like when we found a groundhog run over in the field or a cat drowned in one of the deep old cattle tanks. It was sad and sickening, and I started to think my family was trying to tell me that my hand was dying, that it stank, and before long we'd all bury it in the garden in a plastic bag that the next spring we'd unearth when my dad took some time away from the real fields to plow up the garden for my mother to plant sweet corn and pumpkins. I imagined us all poking my rotted hand with a stick, just like we did the other dead things we found as my dad waved us out of the way before letting the silver shears down for the last swipe, to make the deep furrow my mother would tell us to place all the excavated, Wonder Bread-ed cadavers in. "Pee-You!!!" we'd say, and never once did it occur to us not to bury things in the garden in a plastic bag that wouldn't biodegrade. I still don't like bread bags.

"Here, put it on," Darren told me as he pushed the bread bag into my good hand. Reluctantly I shimmied the bag down over my bandages. He helped me tie it around my wrist with a twisty. I wanted to protest, to whine some, but I knew what it would mean, and I wasn't about to risk not having my bevy of runt pigs all to myself. Once the dying hand was bagged up real good, the white faces of those smiling punk Wonder Bread kids on top, Darren spoke quickly and clearly to me, his brown eyes locked solidly on mine so I'd get that the message was for real: this was sober stuff.

"Now, you've got to keep a heat lamp on them or they'll die right away. Remember, these pigs keep warm beside a five-hun-dred-pound mother and they've not got that now." He pulled me by the arm like we were under some strident time constraint. I assumed it was because he feared our father or grandfather would find us out, or the fact that we'd essentially stolen both animal and feed from our own family. It made my brother sweaty, in his hurry to instruct me and get back to his regular chores.

He led me into one of the four wooden rooms. He'd put up a new gate made from tossed-away boards; it hung on old hinges pried from some other shed on the farm. It swung open when he unlatched a new silver T-lock that he'd bought with his own money at some point. He wore a pair of Levi's so dark blue they appeared black. At night, after the work had been done and he'd bathed and was lying on the bed in the room we shared, I would notice on his white thighs blue stains from his new jeans; the dye coaxed out from all the sweat it took to haul manure, steal runt piglets for a little brother with a bad hand, and run from tractor to tractor looking for misplaced tools needed to take care of the day's constant deluge of repairs. He also wore a Van Halen T-shirt, not something he normally would have donned, but now he was a teenager and was trying to find a way to fit in, to balance our farmer's uniforms with what the suburban kids were into. It would be a battle for both of us as we longed for eight-track players and a huge satellite dish, simple video games that plugged into your television, and all the rest of the garb, music, and gadgets that our counterparts at school, whose parents didn't cash-rent for a living, had at their disposal and talked about at length.

We wanted to make our parents' dreams come true, to toil alongside them to eventually own their own farm, but we were stuck as well, crammed into the middle of two worlds that were vastly different, the wants of one generation in a tug-of-war with another, even worse, with ourselves. We wanted to become great Agri-Kings of the Midwest but with all the perks of the suburban lifestyle too. It would prove to be our undoing, a whole generation of farm kids who now are bankers and grocery store managers, salesmen, and teachers, middle-aged people all across the Midwest who still remember wanting badly for Christmas a Walkman but who still needed coveralls for chores. I see them when I travel through the Midwest, farm kids now aged, standing behind bank-teller windows or checking me out in a bookstore, their faces recognizable by the grief in their pallid eyes; it's a shared secret we hold, a guilt that we never stayed put on a farm somewhere. I see them looking back at me, saying, "Sometimes I wish I could go back, don't you?"

In Chicago, Indy, Detroit, and Minneapolis I've seen them, members of my generation, as much from a certain place as a time and culture, cash renters, never owners, moved from four hundred acres into townhomes and loft apartments, trying their best to forget robust childhoods filled with work and animals and big families to become comfortable with the fact that they were only kids trying to make it happen, not adults. We wanted finished basements with shag carpet and a brown bumper pool table with green felt instead of the dank, wet, ancient cellars under our temporary farmhouses where we hid out with our whole manure-stinking families during tornado warnings, the dogs with us, maybe even a prized boar or two, protected from the storm. Sometimes I want to go back there and be holed up during a horrific downpour with the other six D's. Huddled together so close we could smell our work boots as if in some exotic leather shop in an international airport. But a memory can become a dangerous thing; sharpened over time it can develop the most exacting of edges, gutting out that part of us that we most wanted to keep intact. In the summer of 1976, though, on our rented farm, all I wanted to do was prove I was a real hog man, not a baby-faced kid whose hand didn't work well enough to farm like my grandfather. It was exquisite irony that the most vulnerable, the most discarded of the farm's creatures would help me move along that path.

In the stall, Darren showed me how to make certain the runt pigs bunched together under the heat lamp, how to ensure they'd stay warm if I remembered to close them off in a small section for just a few more days. It was summer, of course, and hot, but the piglets were sick and supposed to die. The loss of body heat, if I let it happen, would take them for sure, he told me.

"It won't be that way if you can get them to eat, put more fat on their bones." He smiled again, and I was grateful the lecture had turned back to fun once more. He pulled something from his back pocket I'd not seen when we were sneaking out to the shed.

"Use this at first to get them to drink." He held up a baby bottle with a tan nipple. It too looked brand-new, something he'd most likely also bought with the loose change he kept in his sock drawer. He snuck the baby bottle into our house like contraband. Who knows what our poor mother would've done had she seen it—a painful reminder she'd never give birth again.

"I made the hole on the end a little bigger." He tipped the bottle toward me so I could see; white milk plopped in rapid drips onto the straw floor.

"That's milk from the refrigerator in here," he said as he shook the bottle. "Don't get caught taking it; they'd be really mad if they knew." Darren handed me the full bottle. "We'll have to figure out later how to get more, but for now give them all a few ounces each and I'll see you tonight at supper."

Darren gave me five and left the shed in a flash. For the first time in my life I felt the awesome responsibility, the heady delight, of getting the chance to save something. I thought Jimmy Carter would be proud, and that's when the name occurred to me. I'd name the smallest, runtiest piglet Peanut. One by one I carefully carried the babies to their new home under the warm heating lamp, the russet light like something the grandparents in Terre Haute might witness at night around their fat Bible on their beautiful Christ table. The pretty red light made the straw crimson and all the runts the same color. When I got all six of them snug under the lamp, I sat down in the straw and rested my back against the wall. I picked up Peanut and held her before my face. She looked drowsy, her tiny eyes batting weakly, the long lashes like the ones on Dana's baby dolls. The little runt shivered, but I couldn't feel her breathing. She was; it was just that she was so tiny, so slight, that what little breath she needed could be

inhaled and exhaled without any more effort than an impercep-
tible blink. I put the nipple to her wet snout and waited for her to
guzzle down some milk. She let the tip touch her mouth without
even making a move. I repositioned Peanut so she could rest
against my chest; it was hard not to use my right hand. Everything
was harder to do, and I learned to utilize my knees and feet to hold
and steady almost anything.

I squirted some milk from the tip onto her nose, and suddenly,
as if she'd been given a radio-controlled command, her fuzzy
snout opened and she sucked from the bottle as if it were as good
as the Pop-Tarts we fought over. I didn't want to pluck the nipple from her hungry mouth, but I remembered what Darren had
told me and placed her back under the light, picked up the next
piglet, and gave him some milk as well. By now they were all making a tiny little chorus of squeals, light and barely audible, not
like their healthy counterparts in the farrowing house, but low
and soft, like the noise I thought butterflies would make.

I fed each runt pig and couldn't believe my luck. I stayed out
in the shed until almost dark. If I could give you one piece of
advice, one thing you simply must do before death, it's this: make
friends with some corporate owner of a huge hog factory in
Florida or North Carolina (the two states that imprison more hogs
each year than anywhere else on the planet) and get him to let
you come over and hold the runt piglets before they're extermi-
nated. Then run off with all that you can carry. Hide out along
some road under a leafy, broad oak tree and cradle those runts
for as long as you can. It will change your life forever.

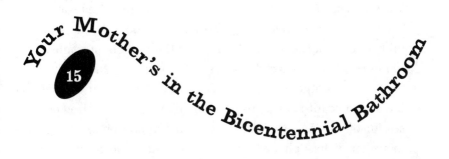

Your Mother's in the Bicentennial Bathroom

15

Early the next morning I was eager to get out to my very own hog shed and check on my litter of throwaways. It was a beautiful dawn. In the front room of the Grady house, orange sunlight slanted in from the tall windows that stretched from the floor to the ceiling. In the winter, we'd cover the long panes with plastic to keep the cold out and the capricious utility bills down. We were always aware of the bills: medical, utility, fertilizer, feed, school clothes. They swarmed about us like gnats, but the bills did more than bug us. They nearly choked off our air, there were so many to try and swat away. It was exhausting for my parents.

I pulled on my work boots in the living room, tucking the laces inside the tops rather than struggle to tie them with my left hand. I could barely wait to get outside and tromp across the wet grass to the hidden shed. My plan was to be up so early that not even Darren would know I was facing my first complete day as a full-fledged hog farmer. I'd schemed in my head before falling asleep how to get more than one bottle of milk for my runts. I could siphon some off from the jug in the fridge for the morning feeding, but what about the afternoon? And night? I knew piglets ate three times a day at their mothers' teats and I wasn't about to let mine get a raw deal. As I stood up to sneak the milk, I heard music coming from the bathroom. Country music. Johnny Cash, to be exact. It was a song I loved, "Boy Named Sue." One of my mother's sisters in Terre Haute had sent an RCA Stereophonic turntable to us the year before. It was a prized possession of the 7 D's. We took turns playing records on it. An enormous set of headphones came with it, puffy and heavy on a child's head; it weighed down our necks unless we propped our heads against the wall to listen. Most desirable of all was to get to take your turn and listen in isolation. I loved listening to Johnny Cash and Glen Campbell, but most of all I played a song by Roger Miller over and over. It was called "Vance" and it was about a boy who should've died at birth but somehow overcame all the odds to become a man. The chorus goes: "Papa, do you become a man at twenty-one?" and Roger would sing, "Age doesn't make a man a man, my son." It was hokey and sentimental, just the kind of lyrics I enjoyed the most. I looked for the turntable beside our beat-up old couch where it usually rested on a pine table my mother's father had made and painted black. It was gone. It had to be in the bathroom as I walked toward the sound of the needle being lifted and placed down once more, so that "Boy Named Sue" could play all over again.

I heard the needle scratch nervously over the starting groove; once and then again two more times Johnny started to croon and was rudely interrupted by an unsteady hand. The drag of the needle over the vinyl popped and squelched the speakers. Finally the song took hold, and the lyrics I loved wailed in the bathroom and reverberated off the walls; I could hear a slight echo and the sound of my mother's strange voice singing along. Before the operation she'd had a beautiful voice, to me anyway, but since her womanly plumbing had been redirected, her normal tone and cadence of speech had become monotone and on the monster-ish side. It reminded me that I'd thought she'd had a lobotomy; her voice was dulled and numb.

I walked to one of two doors that led to our only bathroom. It was July 1, 1976, three days away from our country's bicen-tennial. As I eased the door open I witnessed my mother on her knees, barefoot and wearing a dress I'd only seen her in once, when she went out with my dad to see the movie *The Towering Inferno,* the only leisurely event I can ever recall them attending as a couple.

I could see she was busy working on the base molding; she was scraping and sanding at the same time. She'd thrust a putty knife along the baseboard and remove a long strip of white paint, like the withered snakeskins we found in the fields, and then toss the knife down to quickly grab up a piece of coarse sandpaper, shoving it along the scarred baseboard as if she were about to push the entire house from its foundation. She seemed angry, her movements were violent and strict. She was letting the molding have it. Dust and paint clung to her arms, and the dizzying scent of paint thinner filled the room. The Cash song was near the end again when she leapt up from the floor and turned to start the song over. When she laid eyes on me, I felt like turning around to run. My hand hurt, and under the gauze I could feel the blood throb like a kettledrum. I was scared of her right then.

"Hi, baby," she said, wiping dust from her round forehead, scotch tape again holding down her ample black bangs, which wanted to curl up rather than lie down straight and behave. She walked around me to the RCA turntable and fumbled again with the needle. She stopped, put her hand on her hip, and sniffled, her back to me. Through tears she choked out, "Dougie, could you stand here and start this song over for your mother whenever it ends?" Her voice thickened with emotion. "She can't seem to get it right." She rambled back to the baseboard and I put the needle on the right groove. I fell for the third-person reference again, looking around the bathroom to see if my real mother was standing nearby, perhaps by the shelf of towels and washrags, the ones so used by the 7 D's that most of them were gauzy thin, like scrim, but she wasn't anywhere to be found.

As if an internal shock had somehow completely changed her, she jumped up again and came and gave me a full, hot hug, careful not to hit my hand, which had happened over and over again; I'd either hit it against a doorjamb or one of my innocent siblings would accidentally ram it while playing.

My mother smelled like the room, hints of fuel and cut pine, and felt too hot. Her hug went on for some time before she pushed back gently and smiled oddly at me, her wide-spaced teeth, weakened by poverty in her childhood, were hidden as quickly as they'd appeared; she clamped her bright pink lips down in a pucker to keep from crying. In an instant she was back to the floor, her dress hitched up to mid-thigh. A mottling of purple bruised dots from her ankles to her knees made me want to take care of her, help her with whatever project she was engaged in now, reckless with her body, letting it take the punishment of work. The song played through one whole time again, and on cue I used my left hand to lift the stereo arm and place it back at the start. I watched her scrape and shove, my worry for her now doubled with the concern for my runts and how I was going to get from the hot bathroom laced with liquorish fumes to the kitchen to filch milk and out to the shed to feed my babies.

The song was halfway through again when my mother stood up and walked toward me slowly, a shy grin on her red-blotched face; I've never seen her look any more vulnerable than right then, like a reluctant child left with a harsh relative, only to be picked up in a few hours by someone else who couldn't care less about the little thing. Sometimes an image can haunt us; that's one of mine. It pops into my mind weekly, along with many others, and I try and swallow and figure out what I am supposed to do with it.

My mother took me by the arm and twisted me around as if taking the lead in a dance where I was expected to twirl under her guidance. Instead, she pointed me so I could see the corner of the bathroom, just off from the tub all 7 D's used to get clean; it had a long, fiery orange flame of rust that shot up from the drain, nearly licking the back splash where a line of gray mold never seemed to go away, even if it was bleached and scrubbed.

Even though I'd already seen her handiwork on the wall, as she turned me to face it she placed her sticky hands over my eyes. Her fingers were splayed so widely that I could still see perfectly except for the thick fleshy bars, scented heavily with bromide and pine dust, lightly pressed against my sockets, her short pinkie tips touching under my nostrils.

"Surprise!" she exclaimed weakly as she withdrew her hands from my face and edged me forward so that I could get a closer look at what she'd apparently been up all night doing. That section of the wall had been sanded and repainted and was now wearing stripes of bright red, white, and blue where a pale peach had been, the same color that still clung to parts of the remaining walls. In perfectly spaced proportions she'd stuck on appliqué stars, silver ones of varying sizes, the biggest ones the size of dinner plates. Over it all she'd tossed gold glitter before the paint had dried, and it shone in the light coming from the shadeless lamp she'd brought with her from the front room. It basically repeated what she'd done in there as soon as the year changed from '75 to '76, but with a few new configurations of paint and glitter.

The record started to play another song. She didn't ask me to go repeat "Sue" again. To a kid, what she'd done was mesmerizing. It was like a fun school art project, gaudy and limitless in the use of supplies. I noticed five unopened bags of silver stars on the floor next to a stack of paint cans and glitter in plastic tubes a yard long. But we were cash renters, and if we'd learned anything about that arrangement it was this: you had to get all changes approved by your landlord. This cardinal law included the house, crop rotation, how many hogs were set for sale, and the prices at which feed was bought and grain was sold. My dad would sometimes say, "We can't take a shit without the landlord wanting half of it."

"Well," she asked, a lingering question mark on her face, "what do you think, sweetie?" She ripped the tape from her bangs and it fell to the floor with some of her dark hair stuck to it. "Your mother's going to get the whole room done," she said, splaying her arms widely to encompass the space, "before the Fourth. Don't tell anyone. It's a surprise. She wants it to be a surprise."

Where we were going to bathe and use the restroom had not occurred to her. She was manic and full of energy. Before I could tell her how pretty I thought the wall was, she was back to work scraping and sanding. I stood and waited for her awhile, wondering if she still wanted me to keep repeating the song, but she didn't say another word, and I snuck out of the bathroom through the other door, grateful to be on my way to the kitchen to fill the baby bottle with milk.

Out across the yard I scrambled full tilt, the sun warming my face as I rushed to the shed to feed my runts. The night before, Darren had checked to make sure I pulled the old door shut tightly and twisted the bailing wire, threaded through the drilled holes on the barn and door, to keep the piglets safe. Now I was so excited, my hand covered in bread bags, that it was difficult to get the wire free to get inside. Finally, after twisting it wildly, I was able to yank the door hard enough to open it a small crack to slide into the shed.

A tang of dust and a whiff of hay clung to the air inside the shed. I was scared to look, but wanted to so badly my hand became a minor concern, secondary in light of the welfare of my runts. They were sick and vulnerable, and I didn't want to see if any of them had died in the night. I covered my eyes the way my mother had covered them minutes ago in the bathroom, big spaces to peek through. I could see the red glow of the heating lamp. Underneath, a pile of little bodies lay motionless; the foster piglets could've been a stone or tin pan, they were so still. I swallowed deeply and pulled my hand from my eyes. I unlatched the door, pointing the baby bottle like it was a gun and I was a burglar sneaking into a house rather than hand-nursing some runt pigs.

I thought for sure they were dead as I took small steps closer and closer. I leaned down to see if they were breathing, but something flashed in the corner of my eye; through the slats in the shed I could see movement outside in the green ragweed. Something prowled back and forth past the gap in the boards, made the light piping through the slats flicker on and off, on and off. I froze, unsure whether to run back to the house or prove somehow that I was responsible and tough. The creature outside the shed slowed its pace, and when I took a terrified step toward the slats and the twinkling ray of light I could make out Joe's fur, blurry tan and black, in motion and hyper.

I was relieved and glad it wasn't some newly spawned beast from The Prairie prepared to take my head back to the caverns of witches and the bedeviled Schwann's man held captive in their devil-worshipping lair. Joe skulked past the shed, his fur coat disappearing into the weeds like Gentle Ben into the swamp. When he yawned a sort of coarse whinny, I could tell he was now retreating, leaving my shed for the deep cornfields and damp pastures of our neighbors. While I worried for him, I just didn't have time; I had to feed my pigs.

I sat down next to the heap of six runts and plucked a white one from the top. He was warm and soft, and I could feel his tiny ribs as I placed the nipple to his lips. His crossed eyes popped open, his little hunched back bobbed up and down as he suckled nearly three ounces before I could pull the bottle from his pink snout. I had to get them more milk; at this rate I'd only be able to feed them once a day, not enough, Darren had told me, if I wanted to keep them alive. I picked up runt after runt and let each drink two ounces of milk, until, on the bottom of the pile, under where all the others had been heaped, lay Peanut. She was not very warm to the touch and her eyes wouldn't open. Dread washed over my chest; blackness clouded my vision.

She's dead, I thought, as I tried to insert the flimsy nipple into her mouth. All at once, Joe appeared again at the crack in the shed. He barked and yapped, dug his paws into the dirt, clods hitting the weeds as he shot it back through his hind legs. The commotion made the other runts scramble into the corner. To my relief, the noise jolted Peanut into a wiggly state. She latched onto the nipple out of sheer happenstance and began sucking. Her tugging at the bottle, draining the last few ounces in less time than it took for Joe to bark twice, told me I'd have to find more milk for them right away. I said, "Joe, stop that or I'll thump your ass." I'd heard Derrick and Darren say that a lot; cussing when I was alone was something I greatly enjoyed. "Joe," I said, a little louder. "Stop that shit right now, you bastard!"

It occurred to me I'd not eaten anything myself as I placed Peanut back with the others in the gold straw. Cereal, I thought.

That's it, I'll use the milk that's always left over in my brothers' and sisters' bowls for my runts. Darren's would be gray with sugar, and they all might have bits of Wheaties in them, but that would work. I felt like I'd discovered plutonium. As I walked back toward the house I cussed at Joe as he whined for me to scratch his ears. "Damn it, Joe, you shithead, watch my hand, boy." He seemed to smile when I reached down and rubbed his neck.

16 Dot Matrix Bills and the Fourth of July

With the impending return of my dad's parents from Terre Haute, Derrick and Darren were enlisted to make sure the farm was running at the optimum level. This meant my father had them hauling manure and spreading it wildly on two patches of old rye behind the barn. They both wore ponchos to keep the shit from getting in their hair or landing in splotches on their bronzed forearms. For two whole days I tried to stay clear of almost everyone in the family. While I still wanted to get back into the main farrowing house to pet all the newborn piglets, I was becoming more and more satisfied with my own hodge-podge litter of castaways.

The girls and my mother, really for the first time, occupied different worlds inside the old farmhouse. My mother worked frantically on the bathroom, transforming it into a shrine of 1976 patriotism, while Dina cared for Dana, playing dolls and baking the dozens of biscuits we ate at nearly every meal. As much as my mother wanted to keep us from seeing what she was doing, it had obviously proved futile. She tried to hint around that we could all do our business in the cornfield right outside the back porch and maybe wash up at the spigot beside the house, but my dad intervened.

"Doris," he said, "Grady's not gonna be real damn pleased about all the decorating you're doing in there anyways. Last thing we need is for him to drive up like he does and see these kids toileting in the corn and naked washing with the hose." She protested. Finally we all settled on a suggestion of hers; for the next two days, until she was through, we were to close our eyes whenever entering the bathroom. Of course we said we would, but it was asking a lot of us kids to not look at something. *Don't look at the streetlights, or you won't be able to see anything at all.* Wabash's long-dead citizens, alive in 1880 and tempted by restriction, would have understood our dilemma, the tease inherit in forbidding a glance.

Like the rest of the family, at the entrance to the bathroom where my mother stood guard like a good border collie, I'd actually cover my eyes, but once inside I'd remove my hand and take it all in. The RCA stereo still stood in the corner, the vacant turntable sometimes rotating unevenly, clicking slightly when I dropped my drawers and inspected the rest of the room. What she'd pulled off in just a few days of manic work was hard to believe. The walls now matched the one little corner she'd shown me. *Look at what your mother's done.* Silver and gold glitter adorned the red, white, and blue paint like stardust floating in a haze along a backdrop of infinite bicentennial space. Above the medicine cabinet she'd placed a clear-backed sticker that read: Don't Tread on Me! Two hissing snakes, coiled and ready to strike if made to pay taxes without some fellow snakes representing them, underlined the slogan. In the corner was a whole stack of unused supplies, and it occurred to me that all of this had to be costing money we really didn't have, and that my father, a thirty-eight-year-old man with five kids and no real idea what was happening to his wife, was simply trying to keep her occupied until she healed.

In fact, in the mail that day arrived something he'd begin to associate with pure dread, an envelope from the hospital, a weird-looking bill inside. Dot matrix printers had just begun to be used only in places like libraries and hospitals. We'd never seen one before. Usually, bills were typewritten warnings of overdue status, or, if the bills were related to farming, blue ink pressed deftly onto a yellow legal pad. As the summer wore on and the hospital bills multiplied, we came to view the dot matrix printouts as evil incarnate; their grayscale letters and digits, their perforations, their cascading length made us sick. To this day, even though it's now rare, whenever I see a dot matrix printout, I look around for the authorities, assuming I'm about to be carted off to debtors' prison, where I'll hook up with the other 6 D's, all of us placed in the same cell for similar civil charges: *Failure to pay this bill can result in further actions.* For years after that summer of 1976, my father's face would wash with dread whenever he plucked one of those damn hospital bills from the envelope. I hate them. Damn them all to hell.

It was the evening of July 4 when the colder temperatures set in. We couldn't believe that the weather reports were right, but the predictions were for temperatures in the mid-forties at night. The corn in the fields had tasseled some, and most of the garden and the rest of the farm was in lush bloom, the flowering soybeans stretched across a wide expanse of acreage like drops of purple paint on a verdant Pollock canvas. The cold front swept down from Canada just days after we'd had to put a great deal of thought into keeping the boars cool in the shade of oak trees next to the fence line; my dad and brothers had sequestered the crabby old men by stretching barbed wire in a huge half-moon under the tree, running temporary steel posts along the same line where the tree limbs cast shadows at the hottest part of the afternoon. Now, as the sun rose on the Fourth, my dad worried helplessly about how the crops would react to such a dramatic change, even if it only lasted one night, a fluke, a gag by Mother Nature herself, the TV anchor told us, right before he turned to his cohort who would be back in a few minutes to examine Jimmy Carter's ever-increasing chances of winning the White House.

I sat up straighter on the sofa when I heard the newsman mention Jimmy. We were all briefly together in the living room, watching the news while my dad laced his work boots, my brothers on either side of him on the other couch. Our mom and the girls were still in their nightgowns. My mother's eyes looked weary, the little puffy brown bulbs underneath them like the backs of field mice. It was odd for all of us to be in the same place at once, taking in the early start to the day. Since my fingers had been mauled I'd pretty much been on my own, and my mother had coped by working endlessly on the bathroom. To my knowledge my father had no idea that Darren had robbed the farrowing house of the disabled pigs; I supposed he had so much on his mind that if I came parading up the steps of the front porch with all six of the runts on leashes he wouldn't have noticed. His head was full of bills, the weather, a hormone-less wife, his old man returning, and a barnful of newborn pigs he surely hoped would make it through to sell in early spring. So when the newsman came back on the television, I was overjoyed to hear him speak directly to me, my father, that is.

"Doug, your brother tells me you like Carter for president. That's a good choice. At least he's done some real work, unlike those other politicians. That's who your grandpa will be voting for, come November. He'd rather eat his own hat than vote for a Republican."

With that he slid past me out of the room with Derrick and Darren in tow, their boots thudding against the bare floors, rumbling like distant thunder until they couldn't be heard anymore. I leapt up from the couch and ran to the window. I watched the men as they strolled across the yard to the tractors. My father turned back quickly and motioned for Darren and Derrick to go ahead and get started. I pressed my face against the window so I could watch him strut back toward the house. My mother and sisters and I could hear the front door screech open. He yelled into the house.

"Doris? We'll see you all tonight to watch the fireworks, no need to make us lunch, we'll work right through and eat a big supper if you don't mind." I looked at my mother. She smiled and silently nodded her head yes. There was a large pause. I could sense my dad still standing at the open door on the other side of the house, waiting for an answer. The girls were busy brushing each other's hair. I shot another glance at my mother. She mimed, "OK" my way. I waited. Finally I yelled back, "OK, dad." My mother clapped her hands, or made the motion anyway; she didn't make a sound.

At the first notion of dark, we all put on our jackets. We were not going into Wabash to watch the fireworks, we never did; we always sat in lawn chairs in the haymow, which rose high above the rest of the farm, towering over the cornfields a good thirty feet. It was like we had our very own private amphitheater. A pair of enormous doors could be pushed open in opposite directions on rusty metal discs that operated along a track not unlike a train's. It was something, to push and shove and finally get those mammoth things open, to look out across the fields and watch the gloaming, all orange and red at the center, pink sneaking around the edges as the sun set in a line of pine scrubs a million miles away. The hogs below us, in the pasture and on the feeding lot, oinking and grunting softly as they bedded down for the night, the crickets and the lightning bugs so thick you'd swear that's all you'd need for the rest of your life in Wabash County. Now, the doors opening to our father's one mighty push, as we settled into our chairs I hid my hand under a quilt as Darren and Derrick, Dina and Dana, and my mom all clapped for my father's Herculean strength, a silly family joke that I was sure my mother didn't remember from last year. I figured the lobotomy had taken it. I was embarrassed that I couldn't clap too, and shoved my hand down further under the blanket.

The fireworks were rumored for months to be the greatest spectacle in Wabash since it first was lighted so long ago. From New Year's Day 1976 the whole country, let alone Wabash, Indiana, had been feverishly planning and arranging for the nation's two-hundredth birthday. The one time I saw my stern grandfather laugh really hard was when Dana asked him if he was there when the country was born. He just about spit out a mouthful of coffee, exposing a grin that seemed so out of place on him that I longed for it to freeze and stay with him forever.

Through the wide-open doors a whiff of a skunk spoor snuck into the haymow. My dad was in a good mood, happy to have the littlest of breaks from all the work and worry. He teased our mother. "Doris," he scolded, implying she'd been the one responsible for the odor. All of us kids burst into laughter, not clapping like when my dad had thrown open the door, and I was relieved not to have to hide that I couldn't do it. I laughed harder, secretly hoping that would become the family tradition.

Suddenly, against the pitch night sky, a burst of red, white, and blue crackled across the darkness, arcing out in all directions, falling like stars into the trees and fields. "Oooooh," we all said in unison. Dana added, "Them's gonna start a fire! Burn up Wabash!" Solidly serious, she worked at a scab on her knee while she sat on my father's lap, uninterested in the other ramparts blasting away against our very own bicentennial portal. It was Sunday, usually just another work day, but since it was the Fourth, we all soaked up the leisure among the purling pigeons roosting on the old hand-hewn beams above our heads. The fireworks went on for another ten minutes before the intermission gave my dad a chance to address us. He walked to the open doors and presented himself to us as if on stage. I'd found my parents' homemade yearbook from Blackhawk High School in Vigo County and in it I'd seen black-and-white photos of my father playing a little part in *Annie Get Your Gun,* his cheeks rouged, hair slicked back, thin as a rail, mascara outlining his smoky eyes, like Elvis, my mother would say. But now, as he prepared to deliver his speech, he carried a paunch at the belt and his hair was in deep recession; his pork-chop sideburns curved down nearly to the corners of his mouth and looked like handles attached to the sides of his face.

"Tomorrow," he announced as he surveyed all his D's sitting obediently before him on lawn chairs, bales of straw as footstools, "your mother will take the girls, Doug," and then looking directly at my oldest brother, "and you, Derrick, to Terre Haute to get your grandparents. Darren will stay here with me to farm." He took a step back toward the open doors, scaring my mother out of her funk for a moment.

"Good Lord, Dan, watch yourself."

"Right," he said, pulling himself back from the brink. He winked at our mother and said, "That first step's a doozy."

Dana and Dina were already chatting about the trip, while Derrick seemed pleased to get to use his newly obtained driver's license, but I felt sick to my stomach. It would mean leaving my runts, and while I was excited to hit the road for Terre Haute, it also meant bringing my grandfather back, which would surely spell the end of my tiny piglet enterprise. He'd always been the one to declare when a boy could stomach the farrowing house, issuing his decision like a magician, Voilà! and you'd be knighted and ushered through the door. But down deep inside I suspected he was never going to allow me in; I'd challenged him when he tried to steal my pigs two years earlier, and I feared he would get his revenge by barring me for life from the place that held all the piglets. He'd think my caring for the runts was ridiculous. I just knew he'd stop it all. I imagined him loudly declaring, "No little piggies for the Pig Boy, no, siree, not on my watch!"

Bursts of colored light arched over my dad's head as he stood in the doorway, his hand on his head, lost in contemplation. Derrick, who was usually shy, gave him a bit of his own medicine, quoting an old favorite phrase of my dad's when more bright shots of fireworks split open the night sky. He said, "You make a better door than you do a window." Our dad would say it to us as he'd wave us out of the way of the television while he watched an IU basketball game. He looked up, worried, and said, "Right," as he went and sat down by our mother. He needed to get her out of the cash-rented farmhouse before she turned the whole thing into a bicentennial museum. His face fell as he fiddled with his nails in the chair next to my mother. He'd gotten a taste of freedom from his parents constantly looking over his shoulder, but now they'd be back in a few short days and the drudgery would return as well.

We watched the fireworks for another twenty minutes. None of us spoke, the sounds of the celebration thundering in the sky accompanying our thoughts. The grand finale started, the rumbling getting louder and louder as the spirit of '76 stole the sky and declared its independence. Our dad stood up again and pointed at Joe, who had snuck up the ladder to the mow (a trick Darren had taught him as a puppy). "Look at that dog." We all turned to look. "He's not even scared of that noise." Our father

looked perplexed. He turned and spoke to our mom. "You remember Princess; hell, she'd be hiding under our legs by now." Princess
was a big white German shepherd I still have dreams about. She
could leap cattle fencing eight feet high without any effort at all.
Our father loved Princess, mostly for her obedience and some
for her ability to work hard without getting into any trouble. Joe,
he felt differently about. Joe was a dog that found trouble everywhere and seemed to prefer screwing off in the fields than helping around the farm. Princess was hit by a car and died, and now
Joe was the family dog. Our mother had wanted to name him
Don or Duke so she could have eight D's, but we outvoted her.

My dad watched Joe for some time as the grand finale finally
ended. Joe just sat idly under Darren's legs and panted. Soon it
was quiet in the haymow; we could hear the soft sounds of the
crickets and the hogs rooting again. We all climbed down from
the mow, straw sticking to our clothes. Darren shot me a look I
understood completely. Not to worry, his eyes told me, I'll take
care of them. But that wasn't the only concern I had. Watching
my dad standing in front of the castle-like haymow doors, I sensed
my mother and I were really screwing things up. Our bodies
were costing money to fix, and the guilt stung. The dot matrix
bills arrived weekly with that awful encryption of impending
doom, the code burrowing into my dad's brain like the worms
that the hogs sometimes got. It was so overwhelming. I thought
my hand would never heal. Ever.

I tried to focus on just one thing as we walked across the paddock together, blankets drooped over our shoulders, my mother
and father holding hands up front with the girls at their side,
Darren and Derrick and me walking silently behind in the fodder of night, an owl hooting from somewhere near the back lane.
I wondered how I could possibly leave my runts, and then I
thought how much I wanted the night to go on and on, never to

end, for us to have stayed up there in the barn forever. I fanta-
sized about my piglets and about meeting Jimmy Carter. I
dreamed my mother well again, and my fingers healed in perfect harmony with my other hand, and my grandparents stay-
ing in Terre Haute. "Doug wants to stay here," I said to myself.
The words felt good as I whispered the sentence over and over
in my head, moving my lips, lightning bugs flashing on, the bleat
of a calf across the road. I repeated them, a little louder, not
enough for my brothers to hear, as we neared the front steps of
the house. "Your brother wants to stay here." The words felt like
medicine, the third person felt right. I stepped inside the house
and went directly to the bicentennial bathroom, where I could
speak out loud to myself without worry. It was like testing out a
new voice at puberty, or rereading a section of a poem, alone.
Loudly, I said, "Your son doesn't want to leave." The words sur-
rounded me in warmth, distancing me from my internal emotions. I felt removed, disconnected from my wounded heart and
the lump in my throat. It was soothing. I looked around at my
mother's handiwork. I thought, *Ahh, no wonder she talks that way.*

17 He's Saying His Runty Good-Byes

I woke up sweaty that night. My hand hurt more than it had before, and I was frightened. Something shivered inside me, a quaking that rumbled all the way up to the space between my ears.

The house was quiet save for my parents' staccato snoring; one would gobble up air on the intake, rattling like a flimsy tailpipe, and the other would push it out in a blubbery exhale, their rhythm spookily similar to that of two woodspeople pushing and pulling a crosscut saw. I got out of bed and slipped down the stairs again to the bathroom. I peed, washed my hands, and looked in the mirror at my face. I'd never really looked at it before. I appeared strange-looking, my hair had gotten blonder and my face seemed fuller than I remembered it; a tinge of brown circled my eyes, a bit like my mother's. I stared at myself for some time before going to the stereo and pulling on the headphones. I put on the record by Roger Miller and found the song "Vance" I loved and played over and over whenever I got a turn. I sat on the bathroom floor and listened to the song about ten times. When I was finished it was nearing dawn. I pulled on Darren's boots and Carhartt jacket from the rack; I liked wearing his clothes, which were too big on me. I figured if I looked older I'd get promoted to the farrowing house sooner.

Outside, the smell of dew on alfalfa swarmed around my entire head; it was an intoxicating mixture of fresh water and green silage, so richly sweet in its earthy aroma I thought I might take a bite from the air itself. The sun was just beginning to rise, a tangerine orb humpbacked on a horizon of etched blue steel, umber along the distant treetops. The calf from the night before bawled again, and from the pasture I could hear the rustle and thrush of bobwhites scratching in the dead fescue. For a moment, my mind returned to the devil worshippers and the Schwann's man's head lying wide-eyed on the front seat of his abandoned truck, but I calmed myself in the third person. *Easy. Take it easy. He's brave. Your son's tough.*

I distracted myself, as I hobbled along the worn path to the shed, by shaking up the two baby bottles of milk. One bottle hadn't been working so well when I last fed my runts. They needed more milk than one bottle would hold, so I'd snooped around in my mother's pantry until I found another baby bottle, a leftover from when Dana still drank Dr. Pepper from it. It was not as nice as the new one my brother had given me; its nipple was cracked and brittle and the inside was stained a walnut color from all the pop, but it would work, and I'd already decided to leave both of them in my shed behind a bale of straw so Darren could feed the runts as efficiently as I did.

I unlatched the door and was about to step into the dark shed when Joe growled at me from the weeds. "Stop that, you son of a bitch," I said, really feeling the power and edge of the cuss words in the pristine quiet of the early morning. I felt bad, though, and spoke more kindly to my dog. "Ah, boy, don't act like that," I cooed. "Come here, boy. Come here." Joe crouched in the weeds and snarled at me. He had something in his mouth; it squirmed gently under the pressure of his teeth. I sat down my baby bottles in the grass and edged forward, holding my bandaged, balled-up hand in the air above my head, which I was supposed to do every hour or so for ten minutes and had mostly forgotten. Holding it up in the air made me feel even more ashamed. I crept closer to the first sprigs of thistle along the perimeter of the vast forest of overgrowth. Joe sat quietly now, his head turned to one side, showing off his menacing profile, teeth and eyes flittering white as I got so close to him I could've reached into the weeds and rubbed his ears the way he liked. It was still too dark to see what he was holding. My heart raced, fearing the worst. Just as I realized I had tears in my eyes, Joe grabbed the body of a poor little squirrel and disappeared altogether into the tall thistle. Later, I'd recognize his presence on that morning as a warning, but right then I simply gave him a little third-person cussing. "Your owner's gonna get you, boy. He's had it with you for sure." The weeds swayed toward the center of the thicket, Joe swimming through them invisibly, I called after him. "He says go to hell!"

Inside the shed, I flounced quickly to the runts' pen. They were up early too, their fuzzy little backs moving up and down like full-grown, normal pigs, rooting the flaxen straw for bits of grain. At first they were spooked as I climbed the cobbled gate and sat down, but soon, one by one, they came to me, so small that the enormous shed seemed ridiculous; they'd be better suited for a small cardboard box, I thought, as I prepared to feed them. They smelled the milk and circled around my thighs and knees to wait their turn. My idea of getting the old milk from the cereal bowls was working; when I asked my mother and sisters to keep it, to pour it into an old jug for me, they never asked why. Maybe they thought I was drinking it or that somehow I was being frugal, willing to use leftover milk on my cereal because my rotten hand had caused so much grief. Either way, I had at least seven bowls of leftover milk each day to use for my runts and sometimes more if one of us got up late at night for a bowl of cereal. Cereal was a big deal in our house; it was cheap, easy, and fast.

Peanut was the last to be fed again. She was too weak to do more than feed from the bottle. When she flashed her eyes open, I witnessed a set of severely crossed eyes. It was a shock when she looked up at me, her tiny head, copple-crowned like a bird's feathery tuft, and those strained slightly filmy eyes fixed on a spot to the left of my head. Her back was humped, I'd noticed that right away, but something in the attention she was getting now made her eyes open up more fully in her funny-looking, sort of smashed-in face. As I watched her sniff at my hand I realized she was blind.

The other runts, each of which I'd named after people I knew, imitating my mother's alliteration, had their own problems to deal with. Two of them, Peggie and Penny, had back legs that didn't work. They dragged their sagging hind legs as if they were pulling a bleak, wheel-less cart. The other three, Don, Denny, and Dave, were woolly as willy-worms with hooves; their only disability was dwarfism—the entire time I took care of the runts, those additional 3 D's were the smallest of all.

The sun was fully up when I showed the runts a picture of Jimmy Carter I'd cut from the newspaper. I'd stayed up all night to spend more time with my runts, and I felt the strange, nervous energy from lack of sleep as I presented the photo to them. Peanut rested in my lap while the others sniffed and rooted at my pudgy body, poking with their tiny snouts at my legs. It tickled and made me laugh as I tried to get them to take the election seriously.

"Look here," I said, speaking to the runts like I'd heard my schoolteachers lecture in class. "This is Jimmy Carter, a farmer, and he's running for President. He's who I'm voting for." My assembly didn't seem the least bit interested in the man as they foraged around me. I placed the photo before one of the 3 D's, and Don, I think it was, tried to chew on Jimmy's face. I jerked the paper away from him, the corner already chewed and swallowed before I could even scold him for his outright act of treason.

"He grows peanuts and likes kids. He's a good smiler and wants people to have jobs. He'll help Mom and Dad get a farm of their own."

I rattled on and on, trying to get the runts to rise up and storm out of the shed to downtown Wabash to sign up to help with the local campaign. It seems silly now, but at that moment it really seemed to me that I could help. As I hid the bottles for Darren and said my good-byes, closing up the shed for what would feel like a lifetime, I decided I would come back home after Terre Haute and go down there myself, get some buttons and stickers and all the leaflets I saw in the window at the Democratic headquarters. It felt awful to walk away from the shed, my runts inside, not knowing how long I'd have to be in Terre Haute with my mother, but my despair was tempered with hope that I could somehow use the runts, like Jimmy's peanuts, to get him elected.

Winesburg, Ohio and Homemade Shirts

18

It was July 5, 1976, around seven A.M. No one noticed when I returned from my shed. Inside the house, the family was abuzz. My father was phoning Terre Haute to let them know Doris, Derrick, Doug, Dina, and Dana were on their way. I needed to hear how long I'd be gone, so I eavesdropped on him while the others sat around the table eating cereal. My mother was packing sandwiches and walking about the kitchen with intensity, jumpy and tired all at once. Darren had already pulled the olive-green tray off the cabinet and filled it with steaming water and Epsom salts for my morning soak. By now, the soaks had become commonplace for my siblings, but I still felt dread in my stomach every time I saw the hot vapors swirling above the dismal plastic Tupperware. I hated the sight of the thing. Along with dot matrix printers, I damn all oversized 1970s-colored plastic trays to hell.

While he poured a mound of sugar onto his Wheaties, Darren soothed me by talking in a conspirator's low tone about where

I'd stowed the bottles away. "Dad just said it's only gonna be three days. Don't worry," he assured me, "you'll be back in a flash. It's just a hop, skip, and a jump to Terre Haute. They're runts; they won't even grow while you're gone." He smirked, and we began to laugh as I placed my hand on the table for him to cut off the gauze, the worst part. I cringed when he plopped my hand into the water, but like a great magician he plucked a minuscule paperback from his Levi's and started to read to me in the same low voice as before. The book was by Zane Grey, and two gunmen were shooting up the streets of Laredo with Colt 45s to take their sister back home to some other faraway town. My hand tingled and stung as Darren read, turning the pages quickly, almost speed-reading. I had to soak it for fifteen minutes morning and night, and it had not gotten any easier since the accident. He knew he had to keep my mind immersed in the text if my hand was to stay immersed in the water.

My father hung up the phone. He wore a thin flannel shirt with the sleeves cut off at the shoulders. His huge biceps twitched as he spoke to us. While he'd always carried a belly above his belt, his upper-body strength was unmatched. He could take a bale of wet hay in each hand, toss them ten feet into the air, and make them land perfectly square on top of a stack in the mow without even grunting.

"They're all ready for you, Doris," he said to my mother. Her back was to him, while she rinsed something at the sink. He went over and turned her around. Darren eased my hand from the Epsom soak and placed it on a kitchen towel with flags on it. My mother had been on the bicentennial kick in a big way, but now she was putting the hobby into overdrive. Darren patted my hand dry with a paper towel and expertly applied the smelly salve to my fingers. I kept my head turned. I no longer needed a pillow to block the view, and the Donald Duck toy I'd chewed on at first seemed way too sissy to request now that I was in charge of my own shrunken hogs. Darren wrapped my fingers quickly. He'd gotten very adept at the task, stretching the gauze around and around my foul hand, securing it all with the stupid bread sack. I wondered who would help me with it once we got to Terre Haute, and how we were going to explain it to my grandfather, who'd surely consider it a jackass mistake. My fingers under the wad of gauze and plastic felt nonexistent, even though they still hurt horribly, even more lately, but beneath all the dressing I thought they were lost. I even hoped for it. Almost every day that summer my little sister had asked when the maggots were coming, as if we were all too foolish to see that they were actually on their way. With a mouthful of cereal, she'd ask, like she did on the very first day, "When them maggots comin'?" When my brothers explained it to her she acted pompous, rolling her eyes as if she knew something bad lurked around the corner.

My dad spoke into my mother's ear as she washed and rewashed a plate at the sink. "Make sure to get back here by Wednesday. I'll need Derrick if we're going to try and replant that back field." He kissed her and left the kitchen. Outdoors, the sound of a tractor revving up rattled the panes of glass above the sink. As my dad passed the open door of the kitchen, he pulled his Funk Seeds hat down more on his head. He and the green tractor disappeared around the barn. Darren stood to follow him, but motioned for me to come with him outside. Under the big walnut tree, morning sunshine dappling his tanned face, he bent down and handed me a book.

"I thought you might want to look at this on the ride to Terre Haute. It's by Sherwood Anderson." The name sounded exotic to me. It was a grown-up's book, thick, with no pictures inside, the spine gold lettered and straight as an arrow. The title was just a name of a city and state: *Winesburg, Ohio.* I turned it over in my one hand, balancing it against my chest. I was embarrassed that I didn't have something to give him. On the spot, I said, "You can have one of my runts if you want." I didn't want him to accept. He smiled at me and rubbed my head, something I both liked and detested.

"No," he said, "but I'll take good care of them, don't worry." He put his cap on and turned to walk toward the paddock. "Look inside," he said. I opened the cover of the book and found an eight-by-ten glossy photo of Jimmy Carter, a portrait with a flag behind him, a golden eagle superimposed above his head. I loved it. Darren was halfway to the gates when he called back to me. "If you can't read all the stories in there, I'll help you when you get back. Try the first one, though, it's about a writer who wants his bed raised up high." I thought he was nuts. He called back one last time as he swung a leg over the white fence, an apologetic expression on his face, his nose wrinkled in disagreement. "Mom signed you up for a parade when you get back. You're going to decorate your bike and ride it. I think she's making you an Uncle Sam outfit to wear in it." He waved and vanished into the barns.

Before I could get all of the last five minutes situated in my head, my mother came out onto the porch. Behind her in a duckling line were Derrick, Dina, and Dana. My oldest brother, sixteen and ready to drive us to Terre Haute, sported a shirt that, simply put, was unsightly—godawful. His face entirely vacant, he stumbled along behind my mother as she presented all three of them to me like a circus act. "Voilà!" she exclaimed. "Look what your mother has done, Dougie. She's made you all matching shirts." She wiped her brow, pushing the loose strands of dark hair out of her eyes. Instead of wearing her hair finely coiffed as usual, bangs taped down, she'd opted for a ponytail. With her hair pulled up in a wad at the back of her head, she looked more like a kid than a mother. Where was this other mother she kept talking about? And why had she made these awful shirts?

My little sister, pleased as a child could be, told me, "Mommy's got one for you too, Dougie!" Derrick remained in shock. The shirts were identical and homemade. My mother had always shown enormous skill in all sorts of craftmaking. She could paint like a folk artist and sew beautiful outfits. Our fellow students at Southwood Elementary envied our specially embroidered pencil bags and finely handcrafted silver-studded jeans, but this, this was an abomination of epic proportions. Derrick's face went from placidly stunned to bewildered and slightly angry, a furrow on his brow like a gridiron.

The shirt my mother offered me, holding it out as if it were holy cloth, energy brimming in her wide eyes, was 100 percent polyester, of course, and it had white stars and red and blue stripes flying off in a million directions. *Gaudy* wouldn't accurately capture the essence of these shirts, nor would *hideous.* The collars were enormous, long triangles that dangled off our shoulders and nearly touched our elbows. Ears might be the best way to describe them; our shirts had floppy ears for collars, more suitable for a stuffed animal than a homemade bicentennial shirt. Dana twirled in a circle, her shirt ears spinning after her, until she got dizzy and went to lean against my mother's thigh.

I took the shirt from my mother's hand. "Thank you," I said. My mother broke in before the words made it out of my mouth. "Your mother has signed you up for the parade when we get back," she beamed. Derrick was tucking the long tails of the shirt into his jeans, trying to make the best of a significantly bad situation. I watched him, hoping my mother's talk about me in a parade would go away. Once he'd gotten all the material stuffed into his waistband, the bulk of the arrangement was so hefty he looked six months with child. It was hard to watch. He untucked it all again and let the shirt dangle to his knees. My mother watched him struggling with the length. "Your mother knew you'd need yours big. She's seen you grow so much this summer."

She turned and left the porch. Dana and Dina seemed to enjoy fiddling with their ear-collars and played around with them while Derrick finally spoke to me. "She put one even longer than this," holding up the bottom of his like an apron, "on Darren's dresser." He looked as if he might vomit. "He's so lucky he doesn't have to come to Terre Haute. You know, she wants us to wear these so when we get there all the cousins can see us."

I took off my shirt and put on my new one and felt the shame he was feeling. Over the course of the summer of 1976 our mother would try her best to get us all into the shirts whenever she could. There was talk of a family photo, but somehow, mercifully, it never happened. Inside the house my mother scurried around, making clattering noises and talking to herself. My shirt fit fine; that is, it wasn't a dress like my big brother's, but I could see the long collar out of the corner of my eyes. Even looking dead straight ahead I had the sense that I could flap the collar like wings and ascend a few feet into the air. Derrick, still in shock, continued talking it out with me. "You ought to see that Uncle Sam thing she's going to make you wear when you ride in the parade." He shuddered. I held up my hand. "What about this?" I asked.

"That won't work," he said. "I mean, she's seen you ride your bike with one hand. Besides, Dad's gonna tell you to do what makes her happy anyway. That suit's got a hat and everything. The outfit is like one of the girls' jumpsuits." I must've looked sick at heart, because Derrick came down off the steps slowly and approached me across the gravel. He put his arm around my shoulders. "Don't worry," he assured me, "we all look stupid. She's already said she wants us to watch you in the parade and wear these." He pointed to his chest. Oh, Lord, I thought, how can this be? Maybe the answer would be in Terre Haute, in our mother's parents' house, the place that was like a church inside, the Holy Land. Terre Haute, Indiana, was Jerusalem to us; that's where religion was, where Jesus was abundant on the walls and church services were held nightly. The strength to endure the shirts had to be there as well. With Derrick's arm around me, I decided I'd make the best of it. My grandparents' house contained that special thick Bible on the table with candles and plaster praying hands and a bowl of red and green mints. We'd receive comfort there before going to retrieve the other set of grandparents at our uncle's farm. I spoke to myself inside my head. *Maybe her parents can calm your mother down. Your mother needs it.*

Finally, after standing outside the house for another ten minutes or so, all four of us finding sticks to dig in the dirt with, my mother exited through the kitchen door to the porch. In her arms she held a bundle of clothes. When she handed them to Derrick she exposed what she was wearing. What appeared at first to be a shirt like ours was really a dress of the same red, white, and blue material, way too short, more like something to be worn in the privacy of the bedroom than anything that should've been worn out-of-doors. Derrick took the stack of clothes, three-day's worth for each of us, and simply turned away, headed toward the station wagon. He'd taken all he could and wasn't about to try to face what was standing on the porch, its white thighs bared way, way, way too much, a pair of huge brown sunglasses overtaking its face, like the ones they wore on the Captain and Tennille show we watched on Monday nights sometimes.

"Mommy," Dana said, "you look like a movie star." My mother smiled and then let out a sob. She knelt down and scooped my little sister up and held her face to face. "Your mother loves you, do you know that?" Dana just stared at her, not yet able to decipher the third-person lingo.

Derrick pulled the car up next to the porch and we all piled inside. My mother sat up front with him. They looked ridiculous, him in his long dress and her in her ultra-short one. I sat at one window, Dina at the other, our little sister wedged between, all of us buckled up safely.

Run, Joe, Run

19

It was after eight thirty when Derrick steered the car cautiously onto Pike Street, headed toward State Road 15. The horizon looked jaundiced, a swirl of gunmetal clouds over the pastures as we passed, dirty yellow underneath. As we turned a sharp corner, I saw a blackbird roosted high above us on a power line. It appeared to be speaking so I looked away. The radio was on, my mother singing along to an Elton John and Kiki Dee tune, one of her favorites. In a raspy voice, lower, then sometimes louder, she sang in perfect syncopation, "Don't go breakin' my, don't go breakin' my, don't go breakin' my heart."

I held the book Darren had given me on my lap, opening the thick cover and peering down at Jimmy's face. My hand was hurting as usual, a thrumming of blood that stopped right in the middle of my fingers as if the ends could no longer accept it, didn't want it there. Derrick swerved the car to avoid a pothole. As we were about to leave the countryside for Wabash, I looked up and saw Joe out the window. He was in a pasture chasing a herd of shoats. I wasn't going to say anything, for fear that it would upset my mother, but Dana spotted him and pointed. She squealed, "Joe, boy!" Derrick braked harshly, causing our heads to whip forward; my mother sat up in her seat and took off her gigantic sunglasses.

"Dad's gonna kill that dog if he gets another call about him," Derrick said, distaste and sadness across his wide face. He thrust his palm onto the center of the steering wheel and let it blare. Joe didn't seem to react; he raced around and around the terrified pigs as they swarmed into a tighter circle. At the center of the hub stood a large sow, jerking her head side to side to try and get a handle on the danger. Derrick blew the horn so long it sounded like a ship. We sat in the car, hoping Joe would be distracted and run off or else notice the car and come running to us, but he didn't.

Derrick popped his door open and leaped out of the car. He shouted at Joe. "Get outta there, boy! Go home, go on, go home!" Joe was in a trance, orbiting the hogs, unable to free himself, connected to the herd by way of sheer gravity. Derrick, now sniffling, jumped the fence, his long, flowing dress-shirt nearly tangling him up, a blur of flag, and ran toward Joe and the swirling pigs. Finally, out of the corner of his eye, Joe caught a glimpse of my brother running at him, screaming for him to get out of our neighbor's field. Joe stalled for a moment, then took off in a dash toward the adjacent road. Like a greyhound, he was running so fast his back paws seemed to hang in the air, touching his front ones in mid-stride. It was beautiful to watch Joe run. The car was quiet as we all watched my big brother try and impact something that was never going to change; we'd all started to realize Joe's bloodthirst, but were in denial. Only my dad seemed to know what we were in for, but even he couldn't bring himself to say it aloud.

Derrick came back to the car, his face mottled red, cheeks

damp. He acted the pissed-off man, but it was clear he was still a child, a teenager, yes; but Joe was the only expensive gift we'd received as a family. We were all hurt by how the dog had turned on us. My brother used the tails of his shirt to wipe his face; there was so much material he could've used the thing to dry off after a shower. He yanked down on the shifter jutting out from the steering column, and we were off again. My mother murmured, "Your mother's sorry, Derrick Allen. She's sorry he's bad." Dana protested, kicked the back of the seat. "He is not, Mommy," she said.

We drove in silence for a few minutes, then Dana squealed again. "Oh, look!" She pointed out my side of the car at Joe racing along in the culvert, the grass as tall as he was, his muscular body winnowing the vast green waves as he plowed through them. Derrick sped up. Joe did too. My brother gave it even more gas, and so did our dog. My mother clapped her hands together, which, before the operation, had been a signal to us to behave. Now it was a show of delight. She was enjoying her teenage son driving like a madman. Joe stayed right with the car, leaping drainage ditches and swerving to miss telephone poles. I'm certain it lasted only under a minute or so, but in the car with the D's the race seemed to go on and on.

Finally Derrick put the pedal to the floor, the engine straining, popping from heat. Joe slowed and then gave up. I unbuckled my seat belt and turned around quickly to look out the back window. Joe seemed to fade away instantly down the long county road, a big stupid ghost. The last I could see of him, he was panting with that stupid smile on his face. With the cornfields on each side of the road, him in the middle on the black tarmac, it could've been a postcard. Dana got free of her seatbelt too, but by the time she got turned around, Joe was no longer visible. She whispered, "Run, Joe, run."

Fear Far from I-465

The Indianapolis 500 was long over with by July 5, but we still thought, since we'd never really been there, that somehow the race car drivers would be waiting for us when we eased onto the 465 bypass. We'd been talking about the Andrettis since we first saw the sign for Indy. My brother told me, "You can't see the Speedway from here, Dougie. It's farther in." He pointed out his window in the general direction of nothing. I was disappointed.

When we worked the river bottoms in late May, clearing brush and removing rocks from the rich soil, our dad would turn the radio up as loud as it would go in the truck and leave the doors wide open so we could hear the race. In my mind, Indianapolis was an elaborate, strange city, full of intricate streets and unbridled wealth, luscious speed, rumored to be tons of fun. I'd heard my brother's friends talk about high school girls misbehaving at a place in the track called the Snake Pit, how they'd gotten drunk and showed complete strangers their tops. I'd hoped to get a glimpse of where the cars blasted around the track so fast that the radio announcers had to scream to tell us who was in the lead.

My mother had dozed off during the last hour of the drive, but when Derrick told her out the side of his mouth that we were at 465, his eyes firmly locked on the four lanes speeding toward downtown and his hands gripped onto the steering wheel, knuckles white, she came to with a vengeance. Hair coming loose in the back, sunglasses dwarfing her powdered nose, she sat up and, thankfully, pulled her short patriotic dress down.

"Are we on 465?" she asked, turning her head like an owl and then reaching quickly to turn down the radio. Derrick had done a fine job of driving as the girls played tic-tac-toe and snacked on chips and I gazed at my picture of Jimmy. I'd also opened the Sherwood Anderson book and read the first little story. I'd been waiting for my mother to wake up so I could ask her about several words I didn't know, but now she seemed preoccupied with the roaring highway.

We rounded each twist and bend on the bypass as if hauling a fragile and unpredictable load of nitroglycerin. Derrick had never driven such a maze of flying semis and abrupt lane changers. A spattering of huge raindrops smacked the windshield like tiny bombs. My mother was not helping the situation. She sat up closer to the window, almost pressing her face into it.

"Look out!" she bellowed, pointing at a group of motorcycles in the left lane she claimed were the Hells Angels. That woke the girls. They rubbed their eyes next to me, Dana already beginning to cry.

The rain started to pour down now, the wipers on the car slapping at the gushing rivulets in a futile attempt to give my brother a decent view of the road. My mother begged him to pull over, to get off the awful bypass until the rain stopped, but Derrick was persistent. With the other vehicles and their seasoned drivers cruising at well over seventy miles per hour, any move he could make in the torrential rain would've gotten us rear-ended and sent flying off onto one of the slippery shoulders and down the deep slope. But that didn't stop my mother from fretting.

"Four sixty-five kills more people each year than murderers," she proclaimed, wringing her hands now, almost thrilled by our poor travel conditions. "You know they don't come along and get these people for days, don't you? After someone dies on 465 they'll stink up their car before the state police come; there's so many of them they just can't get to everybody in time."

This got us all significantly concerned. Dana started crying more loudly while Dina tried to soothe her by brushing the bangs back from her sweaty forehead. I took the picture of Jimmy out again and tried to invoke his wisdom and protection. I said a small prayer over his gleaming teeth. When the rain began to ease several miles down the road, I was certain Jimmy Carter was the one to credit.

At the exit for I-70 the sun came out, lacing everything we passed in silver. Dana quit crying as quickly as a doll turned right-side up. Derrick increased our speed and let his hands return to normal on the wheel. We eased off the bypass and onto 70 without any problems at all. My mother said calmly, as if she hadn't just scared the living crap out of us, "Let's stop and get gas and something to drink." She flipped down the visor and pulled a tiny lipstick from her purse, the kind that came in little white capsules so small the girls used them on their baby dolls.

The gas station we stopped at was rundown and stank of oil and urine. The bathrooms at the back didn't have doors that closed all the way; the metal hinges seemed to keep them from shutting. My mother and the girls went first while I guarded their door. Derrick was busy at the hot fuel pumps, filling the brown station wagon with gas. Outside the door to the women's restroom

I could hear first each of the girls pee and then my mother. I held my bread-sacked hand in the air like the doctor had told me to. If I was going to have to be away from my runts, I decided I'd use the time to heal myself with a greater level of dedication, to prepare my hand for when I returned to the farm.

I daydreamed while waiting on the women. I imagined my grandfather Crandell giving me holy hell for trying to keep the runts alive, for being such a fool as to touch a piece of farm machinery, for getting my hand butchered. In my fantasy outside the smelliest gas station in the world, I sat him down and talked it through with him like Jimmy would do. I was mumbling to myself when a man walked up to me out of nowhere like magic from behind a torn-up dumpster, not homeless, but definitely high. He was in his early twenties, dressed ridiculously in love beads, a suede vest, and bell-bottom jeans as large as dress hoops. He wore his hair down past his shoulders and had peace signs all over his clothes, some painted, others buttons. He approached me and spoke.

"Whatcha doin', little man? Guardin' the door for some chicas?" He smiled a bright white Mr. Ed face and put his hand out for me to give him five. I was confused and awkwardly slapped his open sweaty palm with my left hand. He began to talk to me about how the world needed more peace and flowers and gave me a pamphlet about a love fest that was slated to go down in the spiritual realm known as the KOA Campground off of Exit 43. At my feet I noticed a decaying field mouse. It'd been dead a long time, the skull and skeleton exposed to the sun, white as milk, a little furry patch next to it on the cement in the perfect outline of his tiny body, like a page from a biology book. The fur made me miss my runts. I wanted this nut to walk away and for us to drive straight back home so I could feed the babies from the bottles.

"What did you do to the paw, little man?" he asked, a real tone of concern in his voice, pointing at my hand raised above my head in the Power to the People position. He didn't seem dangerous or even out for something, just a high guy in the back of a gas station trying to get people to come to something he'd apparently organized. I walked over to the furry spot on the sidewalk and used the tip of my boot to scrape it off. A rich, musky scent of death wafted up from the concrete, a smell that reminded me of the saddest moments on the farm. The time a little goat died in a shed after eating paint; the whole litter of baby pigs drowned in a ditch after a storm. I kicked at the crisp mouse carcass, a bulge of anger in my throat. The man said, "Sick, man," pointing at the dead mouse.

In a flash I was back at the door, guarding it, concerned that my uneasiness with the man had left the female D's in danger. I was about to answer the man's question regarding my hand when my mother pushed the door to the bathroom open, nearly knocking me off the concrete ledge. The guy looked at her and my sisters and smiled that horsy grin again. Derrick came around the side of the building in a full stride, walking as if his thick thighs would flame up under his jeans. The guy instinctively backed off and passed my brother without looking at him. My mother said, "You know, kids, your mother thinks he's a hippie. She saw a whole herd of them last year at the state fair with your father." The girls squealed. Derrick said, "Come on, it's getting late. Let's get back on the road." He stood before us in his long, long hot shirt, the sun beating down on all of our matching clothes until my mother nodded her head and began to sing. *Don't go breakin' my, don't go breakin' my, don't go breakin' my heart.* She had a beautiful voice. We thought she could've been Loretta Lynn. My little sister told her so as we walked away from the stink. "Sing it, Loretta," she cried, and we all laughed, all the way back inside the car and on our way to Terre Haute.

Derrick had used some money my dad had given him to pay

151

for the gas and buy us each a hot dog, a family-size bag of chips, and Dr. Peppers. Oh, how the 7 D's loved their Dr. Pepper. At home, our mother always put the tall glass bottles in the freezer for a bit whenever she brought home a batch from Clark's grocery. To us it seemed like pure decadence as the cold chunks trailed down our throats after a big bite of fried chicken.

For the next twenty minutes of the trip we were in heaven. The radio was on, playing all the songs our mother loved to sing, and with the windows down the smell of clover and diesel fuel blended so that our heads were as light as the hippie's. We sang along with our mother and ate our hot dogs, then the sandwiches she'd packed. It was a road trip, a bona fide escape from routine, and, while I hadn't wanted to go, right then, with the first taste of what the road can do for a person—the changing landscape, exotic faces passing by in vehicles of all makes and models, the sense of freedom careening carefree down the road to another place, that intermittent feeling of both being away and getting close—I was delighted to be in the car.

Dana made her kewpie doll dance on the seat in front of her as the radio blared England Dan and John Ford Coley's "I'd Really Love to See You Tonight." We passed fields of crops, which Derrick made comments about. He'd say, "Dad would love a place like that wouldn't he? Just look at how their barns are all the same color with white trim." Or "That was an Allis Chambers just like the one Dad wants when we get our own farm." My mother didn't seem to hear him, but I couldn't stop listening to his commentary. While it had brought me out of our silliness, I saw it as a way to talk with Derrick and seem serious about the future of our farming, too. I spotted a herd of Black Angus cattle dotting the far-off fence lines of several recurring pastures. The same exact image seemed to flash by us as we drove, popping up again and again. It was a huge corporate farm, thousands of acres, one of the first of its kind. Its form fit its function: rural factory-like sprawl, designed to take over all the little farmers like us even before we could save enough to buy one of the minuscule homesteads they were gobbling up. When we finally passed the last section of verdant plat, I remarked at how our dad would love to own a herd like that.

"No cattle," Derrick said over his shoulder, as if I should've known better. "We're going to raise purebred Landrace hogs when we get our own farm." He said it slowly and clearly for me, so I could get it right when I parroted it at the dinner table.

Derrick drove until we were out of sight of everything. The farms were gone, only the hilly ribbon of highway stretched infinitely before us; the rolling pavement gleamed, washed out, almost white, the bright yellow center lines visible for what looked like forever. The song on the radio ended and my mother inched forward to turn down the commercial. For a moment she became utterly lucid. She took off her sunglasses and said, "Do you kids hear that?"

We all recognized that her coherence was something to pay attention to. For all of her strangeness in the summer of '76, Doris Crandell was nothing if not a mother trying her best. Yes, she was on a roller coaster of emotions, her body irreversibly cut up, but our mother never lost her intention to be a caring and loving presence. That she fell short at times wasn't due to any intrinsic maternal flaw; the blame for that rested with the physicians who'd determined that the best course of action for a thirty-five-year-old woman with five kids was to gut her reproductive system and then have the gall to bill us under the cryptogram of a matrix of dots.

Derrick slowed the car down to fifty miles per hour. I leaned over his shoulder, watched the orange speedometer needle sluggishly decline to forty, thirty, twenty, as we slowly eased off the road onto the wide shoulder. The slope down into the ditch looked safe, not treacherous like the ones off the devilish 465 bypass. The wheels crunched on gravel under the chassis. My mother perched in the seat next to Derrick, her head tilted to hear whatever it was. I half expected her to laugh it off, act as if she'd heard a voice telling her to say what she had.

The car stopped. We all held our heads at an angle like our mother, listening. I thought I could hear Joe barking, my runts oinking, and the crisp, horrible sound of my father opening bills at the kitchen table, his heart sinking as he unfolded yet another sheath of cruel paper.

Something sounded like my grandmother's coffeepot percolating. A plume rose from the hood of the car, and our view was quickly enveloped in a fog of hot steam. My little sister pointed. "I bet that's it, Mommy. You heard the car sweating." She shook her head in disbelief that we'd stopped because of something so natural. Dana sat back in her seat, told my brother to let the car breathe a little while.

As quickly as my mother had become rational tuned in to the noise, she slipped back. She put her face in her hands and sobbed. I unbuckled my seat belt and climbed out of the car with Derrick to inspect under the hood. It was hot outside, and the air smelled of exhaust and rubber. Chunks of tread from the roaring semis were strewn along the shoulder, deformed cradles of blackness.

Derrick waved the steam out of his face and told me not to touch anything. A car blazed past us and honked. "Nice shirts!" a kid yelled, mocking us with his hand over his heart, flipping us off with the other. I envied the kid right then; he had two hands to use. I forced myself to look at mine, and back at Derrick's as he gingerly wiggled the colorful wires around the battery. I still do that: look at people's hands, mostly men's. Derrick's looked put together well, nimble and strong, capable of deft touch and tactile inspection. My right one was a rotten hunk hidden away. Over the noise of the road I heard blackbirds. I turned to look at the ditch, but nothing was there. I tilted my head to the sky and saw only the glaring sun, a few fast-moving puffy clouds. No blackbirds but in my head. I smelled the death of the mouse from the gas station and thought it had come along with me on the end of my boot, but it smelled too strong for that. I glanced at the edge of the shoulder where gravel gave way to sprouts of crabgrass and spotted a woolly lump lying face up, teeth bared to the sky; a dead groundhog was what gave off the thick stink of rot. I looked away and didn't point it out to my brother, who now had black grease on his perfect hands and a sweat bead glistening on his forehead. He looked like a smaller version of my father, not entirely filled out yet, but definitely of the same build.

"It's no use," Derrick said. "It's gotta be the coolant. The radiator is so hot I can't open it." His voiced trembled. He pulled me with him back to the car and I got in my seat again. It looked like we were going to go ahead and drive it anyway. Dana had climbed up front. Our mother was filing her fingernails, taking a break every so often to tickle Dana's feet.

"Mom," Derrick said, "the car is overheated. I can't get the radiator cap off." He paused and watched her. She appeared to be hardly listening to him. Dana was giggling. My mother cheerily looked up at him as she put her file away and patted my little sister's butt to indicate she should get in the back. "I know what to do," she said confidently. She popped open her door and got out, strode out in front of the steaming hood, and walked to the edge of the road. We all watched her as she posed herself. Our mother, in her short, jingoistic dress of stars and stripes, a larger silver star right smack dab on her derriere, stuck out her thumb, jutted her hip, and tried to get us a hitchhike. A livestock truck blew past, dust and exhaust kicking up all around her, the dress billowing off her thighs to our utter embarrassment.

"Shit," Derrick said, as our mother yelled over her shoulder in our direction. "Your mother saw some hippies doing this when your dad and her went to Marion last month." She held her thumb over her head, a strange position that gave the impression that she was attached to an invisible rope in the sky, a marionette in serious need of a wardrobe change.

In the car our sisters scolded Derrick, telling him they were going to tell on his cursing. He ignored them and instead talked to me. "Dougie, be careful, but go out there and see if you can get her to come back to the car. She might do it if you ask her." Dutifully I crawled out of the car again and approached her slowly. She smiled at me proudly, clearly reveling in the moment.

"Your mother's going to get us a ride. She's going to get us to Terre Haute."

"Come back in the car," I begged her, but she was pumping her thumb above her head, deaf to my insistence. A tan pickup truck with a white band down the sides flew past us, the bearded man inside looking excited when he craned his head to look at my mother. The truck braked harshly up the road and U-turned off the highway and into the grassy divider, floored it onto the opposite lanes, tires chirping, and plopped down again into the grass to ease back onto the highway in our direction. He pulled up next to us. My mother told me to get back into the car. As I was getting in, Derrick got out. The girls and I watched as Derrick and my mother talked to the man. He had on a white T-shirt and tight blue jeans, a big black mustache across his lip like an iron bar. He looked like the actor Pat Harrington who played Schneider on *One Day at a Time*. But this guy had tattoos on his neck and a fierce look in his eyes. He shook Derrick's hand with a lot of gusto, and while he talked he eyed our mother. Inside the car it was like a silent movie, all their movements exaggerated and jerky. My mother still had her thumb stuck out, but it was hanging absentmindedly at her hip.

Derrick got in the passenger side of the truck and shut the door. He opened it again to pull his long shirt into the cab. His face showed reticence, a look of shyness about having been so quickly handed over. Derrick looked like he was being sold off like a hog at auction. He was somebody else's now, free for the taking. I thought he was going to resist, but even with my coaxing him not to leave in my head, trying to send him a message, he was driven away. In a blur of motion they were gone, my mother standing in the hot dust waving and waving until the other cars shooting by began honking and waving back to her. Slumped, dejection on her round face, she walked back to the car and slowly climbed inside. I clutched my book closely to my chest, scared at seeing my brother disappear, scared even more that my mother had arranged it. Dana spoke. "Why'd that man take Derrick?"

My mother began a confessional that left us all in tears and on the brink of total terror. "Your mother shouldn't have done what she just did. She should've waited for an older couple." She wasn't crying, only taking long, rattling breaths between her sentences, pausing to gain momentum for her next admission.

"That man told your mother he'd take care of your brother. I hope he was being honest with your mother. She's seen his type before. Who knows what he'll do to your brother."

Apparently, the plan was for Derrick to go with the man to the next exit and get a tow truck to come back to us and haul the car to a repair station, but our mother didn't tell us that; we only found out later. Fifteen minutes passed, then a half hour. At the hour mark another man in a truck pulled up alongside the car. My mother had been silent for a while, but when she saw the older, gentler-looking man get out of his truck, a pocket protector with a row of pens clipped to his left breast, she instructed us all to lock our doors.

"Come on, lock up. Do it! Your mother's not going to make the same mistake twice," she insisted. Dana started to whimper. My mother popped up from her seat and lurched across to the driver's side and slammed her palm down on the silver golf-tee lock. She told us all to sit still. The old man pecked on the window.

"You alright in there, ma'am?" he said in a measured voice. "Need me to call someone?" My mother acted like he wasn't there, and we imitated her. She started talking aloud again, telling us about death now.

"Your mother lost her first three babies. Two miscarriages and poor baby Brenda. Brenda was just two days old when she died. She was a beautiful baby. She had the tiniest hands and feet your mother ever saw. If we ever get to Terre Haute your mother will show you Brenda's grave. The marker has a little lamb on it. Your mother and dad made it." We'd known about our oldest sister, the one born before Derrick, premature, but it was a shock to hear her name in the car on the side of the road.

The man walked around the car, half crouched down, trying to get a fix on what was happening. He stepped cautiously up and down, his purposeful stance becoming creepy. He appeared to be stalking us. He knocked again on the window. "Ma'am, you in need of assistance?" His cartoonish Indiana accent made him sound like an attendant on a psych ward. My mother's voice got louder and louder as she worked mightily to drown the man's question out. We wanted him to leave us alone; one man taking one of our D's was enough. We weren't about to let it happen a second time, even if our mother was nearly as creepy as the strange man as she yelled about our dead sister.

"Your mother," she blared as if in a noisy factory, "your mother loved that baby Brenda so much. Just like she does all of you. Even the babies that went down the drain, the ones she miscarried." She went on but I was stuck on the word she used. *Miscarried. Miscarried.* I repeated it over and over in my head. A mistake on her part? Had she simply not handled them right in her womb? Dropped them? I allowed myself at that moment, with the old man still pacing around the car, my mother's voice as loud as it could go, the girls now crying, my own chest heaving, to try and become my other mother, the third-person one Doris kept referring to. I tried to feel her hurt. I closed my eyes and imagined where she lived, why she was reporting through Doris all that was troubling her. *Your mother's so tired. Your mother's so sick.* But it was no use; I was scared and about to snap like the girls. I pushed my feet into the back of the seat and listened to my mother hollering again.

"She's not going to let that man hurt us. You mother's right here, girls. That's right. Your mother's right here and let's play a game. Let's play a game with your mother. Dougie, you go first. Say a word and your mother will say one, and then the girls will say one; and we'll just keep going around and around until we have some silly story going."

I liked the sound of that; I liked that idea a lot. The old man shrugged his shoulders and peeked inside the car one more time. His face was in the middle of my mother's window. She saw us looking over her shoulder at him and quickly turned from us, righting herself so that she was face-to-face with him.

"Boo!" she screamed, and the man blinked.

"Boo! Boo!" she yelled again. The man's face contorted. A spasmodic grin blinked on and off, forcing his feet to carry him away from this crazy woman and back like lightning to the front seat of his truck. His tires spit gravel at our hood. Our mother turned back to us, her face red, laughing so hard she seemed to have forgotten how to breathe. It was a wonderful respite from our terror, but it also added to the pendulum of fear and happiness, loss and gain, the ever-changing landscape of our family's deferred dreams, up one minute and down the next, that we'd become accustomed to, even embraced. We laughed along with her until our sides hurt and Dana began gagging, half on tears, half from laughter.

"Go on, Dougie," my mother said, her mascara smeared over her cheekbones like bruises.

I recall saying something to start the game. I'm sure it was an everyday term, but it hasn't stayed with me; what has, though, are my sisters' words. "Baby," Dana said. "Doll," Dina cried. Then it was my turn again. I said, "Grotesque." My mother looked startled, and somehow she tuned in, right there in the shipwrecked car, our brother gone off with a stranger, the afternoon wearing on, getting hotter and colder all at once.

"Don't say that about your fingers, Dougie. Your mother doesn't think they're gross."

She turned to the girls, her chin on the seat, looking more like a babysitter than a mother. "Do you girls think they're gross?" They shook their heads no. "See?" she whispered. "If your mother doesn't and they don't, then that's that." The game we were playing stopped right then.

Behind our car a large tow truck honked loudly. My mother and the girls all turned quickly to see Derrick getting out of the passenger side, a glass bottle of Mountain Dew in his hand, another five in a carton he carried at his hip. I looked in the rearview mirror and watched as his bottom half strode toward the car. His patriotic shirt looked wet. When he approached my mother's side, her rolling down the window so fast it made a funny gaseous sound, his bangs were wet, too. She pulled his head inside the car and buried his face in her chest.

"Oh, thank God. We thought they'd lopped your head off or something." She pelted him with loud smooches and we all tried to get over the seat to hug him, too. He was embarrassed and pushed us back. He was never the same after that. Being sent off with a total stranger down the treacherous highway had marked him. He'd never been completely sure of himself, never, but my oldest brother seemed from then on to regard the world as an unpredictable place. God knows what happened to him, maybe nothing, or maybe something awful; he'd been gone for nearly four hours. Whatever did happen made him more meek and less trusting. He has the biggest brown bovine eyes of all of the 7 D's and I thought, as we waited for the man to hook us up to the tow truck, I saw them misty and shaken, unable to show us what he'd seen.

If Thy Hand Offends Thee, Cut It Off

21

The house I woke up in felt like a church. When I opened my eyes there were rays of silvery light shafting in from the tall windows and on the walls four sets of praying hands, each in a different shade of peach, were arranged in a perfect circle. In the center of them a long black cross hung heavily; its weight seemed to press into the Sheetrock. The room I'd slept in smelled of rain. The carpet underneath a sleeping bag I'd never seen before felt thick and cushy. I rolled onto my side. Derrick snored on a pallet next to me. The few hairs on his chest trembled in the air blowing across us from the box fan propped up on a high-backed ladder chair. My hand hurt, so I pulled it from under the sheet and held it in the air. The house was quiet. I let my mind play over what had happened the evening before. I thought of my book and the picture of Jimmy; I sat up, arm over my head, and searched the room for it. Sitting on a stack of our clothes, the book looked misused. I got up quietly and retrieved it, crawled back under the smiley-face sheet. I opened it to make certain Jimmy was still there. Now I could go back to replaying the images in my head.

After the car had been towed to the service station, my mother's sister Jean and her husband Vern came and carted us the rest of the way to Terre Haute. They were my favorite aunt and uncle because they liked to laugh. Uncle Vern played practical jokes and told stories that always seemed to draw uncontrollable laughter from the adults. He sometimes would draw faces on his chin with Aunt Jean's lipstick, then sit in a chair upside down, legs and feet dangling over the back. He'd place a kitchen towel over his entire face, leaving only his chin and mouth exposed. His head would hang over the edge, making the bottom of his chin look like the top of a little man's head. He'd sing a little Navy song or tell one-liners that I didn't understand. Sometimes he'd just carry on a regular conversation. One time it made me pee my pants a little. Aunt Jean once went out to dinner with us and upon getting out of the car began laughing so hard I thought she'd split in two. At my mother's continual insistence, Aunt Jean finally choked out that her pants were on backward. We got back inside the car and laughed until the windows fogged up.

My mother's parents lived in a simple house off a county road on land that had been owned by the Maumee Coal Company, the company my grandfather Basil Ellis worked for. When my mother was thirteen they moved into the house they'd all helped build. She and her sisters pulled the nails from wooden train cars the coal company had given to my grandfather and they used the lumber to build most of the house. The modest little structure was embedded among the quarries and man-made hills fashioned by a generation of coal miners before my grandfather had gone to work for the company. Several acres of pasture accompanied the house, a fenced-in area for horses, a small stable, and a grove of pine trees in the back that smelled like heaven. My mother's mother, Enid Ellis, planted wildflowers and shrubs in interesting islands throughout the large yard. She'd mix peonies into a bed of irises, along with a few mulberry bushes and too many birdhouses. She loved birds and cats, and could never understand why they didn't get along. Basil was tall and slender and she was short and had kyphosis; the hump on her small back rolled forward, making her appear as if she hadn't a neck. She was sweet and quiet, not at all like my dad's parents, and reminded me immediately of my little runts back home. I replayed the evening before all over again in my head as I lay on the floor, mist falling outside, the sky dark with clouds, and a thunderstorm roiling in the distance. God's hungry tummy, Grandma Enid would say.

It was my mother's idea to have me dress up silly and go to their front door once we got into Terre Haute. She thought they'd love the surprise, but it didn't work. She and her sister dressed me up in my mother's gigantic glasses and Derrick's long shirt; we traded in the back of the car and I know he was relieved that mine did not fit, allowing him to change into a simple white Fruit of the Loom.

They put blush on my cheeks, something I didn't mind. It made me feel like I was filling a minor part in a school play. In fact, I was a willing participant in the prank, only afterward did it feel bad. I wore a seed corn cap pulled tightly down over my ears as well. With the entire outfit on I looked like a midget with sunburned cheeks.

The plan was I would be dropped off at the end of their gravel lane, walk up to their screen door and knock, then ask for Enid. I was to ask to be fed a meal, and she would assume I was a vagrant. She would always say, "Don't ever say no to someone who asks for food. It's Jesus. All of the poor people asking for food, that's Jesus. So if you say no, you're telling Jesus you won't feed him."

After I was seated at the table in the house, my mother and sisters and Aunt Jean and her husband would rush in, laughing and joking, as I pulled off the glasses and cap to expose that it was her grandson Doug from Wabash she'd just served up some holy grub to, but I couldn't do it. At the bend in the lane, I started feeling foolish, a little like we might be making fun of Jesus or midgets or Enid, so I pulled off the cap and glasses and shoved them in my back pocket, and wiped the blush off my cheeks with Derrick's long shirttails. I would just appear as myself, let her hug me tightly, breathe in her weak perfume, and watch her get tears in her eyes. At their door I knocked, anxious to see them, and feeling better about it; the others would ask why I chickened out, and I was prepared to answer, to tell them how I thought it was mean to go through with it.

At the screen door I tapped again with my knuckles, hiding my plastic-wrapped and gauze-bundled hand behind my back. Grandma Enid came to the door. Through the screen a haze of light shone over her figure; it made a tiny, humped silhouette inside the door. Her small, veined hand reached for the knob. "Come in," she said softly. She didn't recognize me. We had not been to Terre Haute in three years, and while my mother sent pictures, it wasn't as if we kids were over at her house like our cousins were on a regular basis. I couldn't continue hiding my hand, and as I sat I saw that she'd noticed it. She gave off a subtle, calming warmth, like a space heater or the glow from a hearth. "Sit down," she said kindly. "Are your parents around?" She looked at me blankly, trying to handle an anonymous, maimed child who'd showed up at her door, she assumed, searching for food. She was a wonderful human being. When I didn't answer, she walked painfully to the kitchen and pulled down a bowl from above the sink. On the verge of crying, I held back, swallowed hard. I didn't want her to be embarrassed at not knowing one of her grandkids so I had to act quickly; I could hear my mother and the others walking in the gravel outside. I pulled out the cap and glasses and put them on in a rush. I blurted out, "Grandma Enid!" She hobbled quickly from the kitchen to the edge of the table, where I sat at the far end.

"It's me, Dougie," I said. She put the bowl down on the table and struggled to get to me. While she hugged me, patting my back, saying how I'd surely pulled one over on her, my mother and sisters and Derrick burst in, my aunt and uncle too, all of them smiling, filled with a sense of frivolity. My uncle Vern poked me in the side a little later, and winked. "You got to work on your timing, Douglas," he smiled.

I watched the whole scene a couple more times in my head, trying to find some clue that my tiny grandmother had realized I'd pulled a switcheroo and put the disguise back on, or if she truly had been hurt by the trick, but as much as I tried, all I could come up with was a feeling of regret. It was silly, but I felt odd knowing what had really happened while they all remained in the dark. I couldn't let it go.

Now, I twisted under the cool sheet, listening to Derrick snore and the thunder get closer. It was very early, around six, and I knew my Grandpa Basil had been up for a couple hours already, feeding and walking his horses. I opened my book and placed Jimmy on the pillow. I began to read Sherwood's story about the grotesques. The rain fell louder on the roof; the smell of cypress from the old railroad cars, which formed the home's skeleton, seeped through the walls and filled the room. I would forever associate the scent of cypress with that tiny church of a house. I dozed off reading for the third time how the writer wanted to raise his bed. I dreamt I was in the sleeping bag hovering over the coal company hills, flying above Grandpa Basil as if on a magic carpet. In little more than a year they'd both be dead, Grandpa Basil from

black lung and tiny little Grandma Enid from despair and lone-
liness, but at that moment as I wavered between sleep and awake,
the water pattering on the roof and gurgling in the eaves, I felt
privy to heaven's plan when I heard the back door creak open
and my grandfather call for his wife. "Dutch," he said, straining
to hush his deep voice so as not to wake us. I could hear her feet
drag on the floor as she went to him. He said with a lilt, "It's
beautiful out here, Dutch. Come on, let's take a walk."

In the late afternoon, Grandpa took Derrick and me into his
room to pick out ties. He'd bought us both dress shirts and the girls
dresses at the K-Mart in Terre Haute. We were getting ready to
attend an evening service at their church, not in their house but
at the real church where they prayed and sang with no more than
twenty others from around the mining hills. He let us pick out
clip-on neckties from his collection, which hung on the back of
his closet door like a nest of snakes. On a hook outside the closet
hung a strop made of dun leather; it had a silver tab where a
pearl-handled straight razor clipped to it to make a complete set.
I snuck a sniff of that strop, letting my nose rest on the pliable
leather so that I left two dots of snot on it like a venom bite. Inside
the closet hung an anatomical diagram of an Arabian horse. It
had arrows pointing to the animal's body and in bold lettering
the words *gaskin,* for the outside lower hip; *fetlock,* for a spot
just above the back of the hoof; *withers,* for the shoulders; and
cannon, for just below the front of the knee. I loved the words;
they seemed cryptic and romantic, full of the kind of insider's
knowledge I thought I could apply to my runts. I made a point of
sneaking into his room later and writing as many of them down
in my journal as I could. I felt like I was stealing words.

I selected a purple tie with white checks. Derrick wanted to
wear my grandfather's twenty-years-of-service tie from Maumee.
It was green and had the coal company's insignia in the center,

little number 20s all over it in yellow print. We all got dressed, my mother in a white dress from her last year living at home, an oddly shaped contraption with leg-of-mutton sleeves, a wasp waist, and brittle lace, somewhat too tight. We left the house and went out to their car. In front of it, Grandpa Basil took a Polaroid of us, my sisters hugging our tiny grandma so hard she bruised, my mother said.

At the church we all sat in one pew. We took it up just by ourselves. The little space was hot and smelled musty, the hymnals so used that the binding flaked off and nettled our noses. It was a thrill to be there. My grandparents kept showing us off and introducing us to all of their fellow church members. An ancient woman with skin drooping off her small frame played the organ, poorly. She hit notes so shrill some people would respectfully, so as not to be noticed, cover their ears. There were no other kids in attendance. It was a church of coal miners who'd survived and the widows of those who hadn't. I couldn't hide my hand and felt awkward trying to shake with my left, but I wanted my grandfather to see I was doing his necktie proud, so I did my best, which usually ended up in more of a circular motion than a pump.

Just as the cacophonous music ended, a man in his forties came in the back door. He was thirty years younger than the rest of the members, and walked with a strained gait. He had cerebral palsy and struggled to speak. He stopped at our pew and put out his twisted hand to shake my grandfather's. After a few moments of speech only my grandpa could understand, he was introduced to us. He repeated each of our names as my grandpa said them, but the only recognizable sound was "d," which came out "duh" over and over until all of our names had been repeated.

"All D's," he struggled to say, and smiled, a strand of drool at the corner of his lips. When he shook my hand I could see his eyes fall on my other one. He lingered on it as the two of us really

169

messed up our handshake. Up on the raised floor the preacher came to the pulpit. Grandpa told the man we'd see him after the service, as he dragged his crooked body down the aisle to the front row. Something inside me ached for that warped walk down the aisle, made me want to go and sit down by him.

The preacher was a coal miner too, part-time, anyway, and he coughed sometimes when he made a deeply felt point. He had the same sooty skin and bleak eyes as my grandfather, the same gravelly voice concocted of coal dust and double shifts. I was disappointed that my grandparents' church wasn't as beautifully adorned as their home. In the church, there was only one cross on the wall, a tiny one, behind the preacher's head, and there were no windows at all. It was a cinder-block building with a red tile roof, nestled in a holler off the same county road as my grandparents' house. We sang two hymns and listened to the preacher talk about the loyalty of the faithful, and when it was over, we mingled with the oldest people I'd ever seen. The preacher left the pulpit only to show up as we left out the back door; I thought it was a magician's trick; I imagined a trapdoor or tunnel under the church like the ones the coal miners worked in day and night.

As we left the front steps, the weak old folks gave us mints and hugged us. They told my mother how clever she was to name us all with D's. The man with cerebral palsy came out of the church last. He shook as he pulled his body down the steps, leaning so hard on the pine handrail that it squeaked under the strain. He came toward us in the gravel, his one foot curled behind the other, dragging dust, his upper body jerking out of his control. I thought he looked like a cowboy thrown from a bronco, but I was sort of scared of him, too. He told everyone good-bye and tried to give my grandpa some money he owed him, but Grandpa Basil said to keep it; he might need to call in a favor one day. The man, whose name I now understood was Ray, handed me a slip of paper. A Bible verse was scrawled on it in black ink, the words kinky but legible.

Mark 9: 43: *If thy hand offend thee, cut it off, it is better for thee to enter into life maimed then having two, to go into Hell, into the fire that never shall be quenched.*

I took the slip of paper and said thank you. It wasn't until I got into the car and Grandpa Basil explained it to me that I came to understand that the man was offering me some type of kinship. We were both maimed, Grandpa said, and Jesus healed people like Ray and me all the time. It was supposed to be comforting, but it was only another confusing idea to me. I wondered if I'd done something to make Jesus mad. It was perplexing, but I knew one thing for sure: I was different from everyone else in the car heading back up the sandy coal mine roads to the house. I didn't think the word *disabled,* but I felt it, right in the middle of my hand, and further in, just above my heart, a pang, homesickness for a place that would never be ours.

Taking the Meringue Ridge Back Home

22

It was nearly nightfall when all the cousins arrived at the house. We'd spent the day riding ponies and playing miniature baseball in the evergreen backyard. The storm had cleared out by noon, the sun bursting free from behind some leftover clouds, cooking the water off the trees and making the whole expanse shimmer and shine. It was a tinsel wonderland. Pine and creosote hung in the air as sweet as something candying on the stove.

At lunch we'd eaten tasty bologna sandwiches with crisp lettuce and ruby red tomatoes plucked off the vines behind the garage, and drank red Kool-Aid from metal glasses of purple, pink, and teal, the condensation on them like dew. I'd dreaded the moment when my mother announced how I'd best get my hand soak underway. The Epsom salts were an embarrassment to me, but in rhythm with their nature, Enid and Basil were more than understanding. They marveled at how brave I was and promised me God had a way of working that made sense once you got to heaven. They said we all got to be perfect up there, that my hand would be normal and so would Ray. By the time the requisite twenty minutes had passed, I was even beginning to feel somewhat proud of myself. They were ideal grandparents in that regard, imperfectly unconditional.

In their house now were all of my cousins from my mother's side. We planned on spending the evening with them, then leaving the next day with Aunt Jean and Uncle Vern to pick up my dad's parents and then on to retrieve our repaired car. When my mother spoke on the phone to our dad, she didn't mention Derrick's joyless ride or his return, and not a word about the old man circling the station wagon; in fact, she was fairly well adjusted from being with her family. It soothed her, made her forget for a while about the disfigurement of her womanly parts and about the farm back in Wabash eating us alive via a heaping plate of unpaid bills. It was nice to see her relaxed, basking in the love of her kin.

My mother is the youngest of her brothers and sisters, by many years. Everyone called her Dory, and they referred to Grandpa Basil as Daddy. All of the cousins were teenagers or in their early twenties. There was Teresa and Denny; Tina, Carla, and Tony; Jimmy, Kim, and Sherry; and finally Cindy and Monte Joe. Monte Joe looked like John Denver to me; I'm not sure why, but somehow I thought he actually was John Denver, and he was hiding out in Terre Haute to take a break from all the stardom. I was weird that way, always thinking somebody I knew was really somebody else. I loved John Denver's alias, though; Monte Joe just sounded so cool, so rough and manly. I thought it would make a good name for a politician, so I wrote it down in my little journal for future reference.

The girl cousins were all beautiful. They had long, straight brown hair with identical auburn highlights. They seemed exotic to me; their perfume thick and flowery, their eyelashes as bountiful as my runt pigs', and they wore clothes that were handstitched and embroidered by my aunts. Like my own mother, theirs too were crafty and capable of making a pile of remnants into imitations of all the current trends. When Derrick woke up in the morning, we had made a pact to hide our bicen shirts (that's what we started calling them) under the mattresses in the spare bedroom. We'd tried to coax the girls into it as well, but we'd been interrupted by our mother calling us to the table for one of Grandma Enid's world-class breakfasts. Luckily, our mother forgot about the shirts, and we were never subjected to the crucifixion of wearing them in front of our relations.

As our cousins fussed over my little sister and talked nonstop to Derrick and Dina, my mother whispered in my ear. "Sorry, Dougie, your mother's thinking it's time to soak your hand again." I felt sick. I begged her, quietly, with my hand cupped around her ear, to be allowed to skip just one, but she wouldn't have it. She whispered in response, also placing her hand around my ear, the noise of the chattering room almost drowning her out, "Nope, I don't want you getting it infected." I complied only because she'd skipped her third-person mother-talk and used the strong, confident pronoun "I."

I got down from the chair and walked into the kitchen to get my tray. I poured the grainy Epsom salts into it and waited for my mother to come and turn the tap water on. The salts in the center of the ugly tray looked so innocent, a little pile of icy snow, but I despised the stuff, thinking its lingering presence was intentional.

As the cousins teased Grandpa Basil about a horse trick he'd messed up at the Saddle Club, my mother tested the water gushing out of the tap, steaming up the kitchen alcove where we were sequestered off from the rest of the family. She had on a peach pantsuit and low black shoes. She smelled like tanning lotion. I looked carefully at her face as she filled the tray with hot water; the deep brown pockets under her eyes seemed to disappear in the dim light.

Head bowed, moping, I trailed behind her into the dining room where the assembly of cousins and aunts and uncles were in a feverish discourse about something. One of my uncles held Dana on his knee, bouncing her lightly as she made her Kewpie crawl in his beard. My mother sat me down at the table and placed the steaming tray in front of me. Darren had been the one to do most of the unbandaging, and I was fearful she'd pull too hard or not distract me enough from the unveiling; that I was having it performed in front of the beautiful cousins didn't help. The hand had been hurting more and more lately, the accident now almost two months old. My mother proved to be just as gentle as Darren; she carefully removed the bread bag and tape and had started to take off the last layer of stained gauze when the room shifted from a soothing ruckus to an eerie stillness. Every-one watched as my mother pulled off the last shred of material, exposing my middle finger. The crowd edged forward to get a closer look. The finger throbbed as my mother turned my hand over. We could see a thin ridge of white down the center, a strand of meringue infection like a bead of caulking. I felt ashamed.

"Oh my," one of my aunts sighed. She quickly got up from her chair and returned in seconds with a brown bottle of hydrogen peroxide. Two of my long-haired cousins came to stand by me, rubbing my shoulders and fussing over me. My aunt poured the liquid over my finger. To my shock, it fizzed up and dripped into the hot Epsom bath. My raw finger was wiped off cautiously, and a second capful of the solution was poured down the length of my finger, fizzing much less this time. Dana came up next to me. "Them maggies come yet?" she asked, and while some of the

adults held back their laughter, my little sister received an expla-
nation from Aunt Jean on how such a thing wasn't possible.

"Change that water," the other aunt said to one of her college-
age daughters, and in a few minutes I was soaking my hand as
if nothing had happened. My mother hadn't cried, grateful, I
think, for someone else's taking charge. This side of my family had
the consideration to go right back to yammering on and on about
everything from how to make banana Jell-o to horses and blister
beetles. One by one, the older, hip cousins approached and talked
to me casually, like I wasn't some deformed Pig Boy but a real-
life younger relative, worthy of their simple interest. When the
discussion turned to politics, I jumped right in, couldn't help
myself. Excited and proud, I retrieved my picture of Jimmy along
with my book and journal. They were passed around the table
after my hand had been wrapped back up and stowed away under
the bread bag.

I talked about Jimmy's peanut farm and how Georgia was
one of the hottest places on earth to farm. In fact, I talked so much
that I wore myself out. Soon, Grandpa Ellis fired up the grill and
set to cooking. In his garage, on the wall, hung a set of enormous
wooden cutlery, a spoon and fork so big they looked like they
belonged to a giant. Sometimes, he'd take the spoon down and pre-
tend to eat with it, and the antic always got rounds of laughter.
As he did it now, the evening air cooling things off, I could see
my mother marvel at his wit; her eyes shone brightly and she
continued smiling way after he placed the huge spoon back on
the wall.

We ate baked beans and hot dogs and drank cans of cherry,
lime, grape, and orange soda. Slowly, the gathering dissipated,
the older cousins heading off for dates and the others leaving
reluctantly with their parents. Dana had fallen asleep in my
mother's lap as I stood next to her. Derrick and Dina were trying

to play croquet in the dark. Monte Joe, the oldest male cousin who I thought was John Denver, handed me my journal and book with Jimmy's picture in it. He was getting ready to leave, his keys jingling in his hand. He rubbed my head and said, "So, Douglas, you gonna be president or a writer?" He disappeared into the dark before I could answer, Grandpa Basil walking him to his car. I heard him kiss my grandfather on the cheek but all I could see were shadows and some pieces of chrome reflecting little bits of light. I can't remember falling asleep that night, but in the morning I knew it was all over. Time to get the other grandparents (and get scolded by Grandpa Fred for my hand) to head back to the farm. Only the promise of seeing the runts again made it bearable.

By mid-morning we had left my mom's parents to go and pick up my dad's. We had a nice breakfast and, while I thought my mother was going to break down when she had to say good-bye to her parents, she held it pretty well together. Maybe it was the strength she'd gotten from being with them for a few days, or perhaps she was worried about my father back on the farm with Darren as his only help, but she hugged them and kissed them as we got into the car with Aunt Jean and Uncle Vern, promising to call as soon as we got back to Wabash, her attitude upbeat. They gave her a Polaroid camera with a box full of film, telling my mother to take lots of pictures of their grandbabies and send them along in the SASE's they also put in the box, all bound together with a thick rubber band.

That morning, before we left, I'd gotten up early and snuck out to their living room to inspect the thick white Bible. I stayed clear of the statue of the she-wolf; it made me feel ashamed. The Bible was colorful and full of Jesus pictures. Bloody on the cross; ascending with gauzy wings; his apostles all at the table eating; the pictures were displayed on thin, crisp sheaves, the ink heavy and nearly fluorescent. I wanted their Bible badly. I flipped through the pages and marveled at all the words, the text so small and compact it seemed it would take a full year for a person to read it, even if he worked at it like a job. I fingered the pages with my left hand, holding my other above, fearful that the ridge of meringue would be back at the next soak. On one page was a black-and-white picture of Christ lying in his tomb. He looked odd to me, a shroud over his midsection, feet projected into space, his stomach and chest much thicker than the Americanized, blue-eyed, and blond one I'd been made to believe was the real thing. Later, in college, when I saw the same picture again, a print of a Mantegna painting, I'd learn that the strange illusion was called a foreshortened figure. I fiddled with the paper between my fingers, focusing so hard on the picture it started to blur, as if veiled by some of my gauze.

Behind me I heard a slight brush of cloth. Grandma Enid stood in the doorway in her nightgown, so small it looked like it might fit Dana. Past her ear, I could see the slight hump of her back. It hurt me to see her there like that, so vulnerable and tiny within the doorframe. I walked over to her and gave her a deep hug; I was just a few inches shorter than she. She walked me to the couch and didn't speak. She was so quiet I couldn't even hear her breathe. In the corner of the room was a little hutch, a curio with mirrored glass and little Christmas lights edging the inside. The whole thing sparkled, making the delicate statues and figurines inside appear doubled. I could see in the center the plastic figures I'd sent them in the mail when I was five. I'd gotten an ark for Christmas one year, a real treat. It had two of every animal in it and an old man and woman, Noah and his wife. For some reason, I pestered my mother until she agreed that I could send the two Weeble-Wobbles to my grandparents in an envelope, its paper pushed to capacity, lumpy and torn.

On the couch, Grandma Enid handed me a locket, a silver one with a rosette pattern, the necklace part made of leather. I opened it and inside was a picture of her and my grandpa; the other oval was blank. She hugged me tightly again and stood, her quilted robe dragging the floor, her poor, poor back puckish as Dana's Kewpie doll. I felt so much love for her it gave me courage. I figured being a grotesque like Ray would be OK; my Grandma Enid was one, my deformed runt pigs were, too. All of us were maimed, the Bible said so, and that was just temporary. In this world, anyway.

At my uncle's farm, we stayed in the car as my mother went to the door of the two-story white house. It was kept meticulous by my aunt; there were flowerbeds lined with perfect rows of blooming perennials, and the gravel drive was raked each night. The lines in the pea rock made the place seem like a golf course. They had a round, red barn and people flocked from all over the state to see it, especially during harvest time. Once we swung from long ropes inside the circular hayloft, and I'd half-hoped we'd be invited to do so now, but it was strictly business on this morning. In the car we played I Spy with Aunt Jean and Uncle Vern, who told my mother there was no way on God's green acre she was going to pay for the car repairs; he'd take care of it.

We watched through the windshield as our other grandparents descended the long set of steps, the porch lined with clay pots overflowing with coiffed vines and tall red houseplants. The first thing we noticed was how Grandpa Fred seemed absolutely different. He'd been sent to Terre Haute to get his doctor-prescribed rest, but now, with my mother on one side and my Uncle Courtney on the other, he appeared frailer, entirely changed. It was as if we'd made a mistake and were picking up a different old man.

Uncle Vern spoke. "Kids, your Grandpa Fred had a slight stroke a week ago. He's fine but he won't be himself." I hung onto those last words. As selfish as it sounds, I was relieved to hear something had intervened to make him different. Had I somehow invoked Jesus from the big white Bible? Or was it just something God planned, like the runts and my maimed hand, Ray's legs and Enid's back? I didn't know where it came from, but we all understood that this new development was a blessing and a damnation all at once. It would mean more bills from a Terre Haute dot matrix, and that was terrifying, but it also carried with it the possibility of a form of parole. My father had always had to consider his parents' sometimes harsh criticism; now, he might be free to try and make the farm and finances work without the fear of someone watching over his every move. He'd gotten plenty of that prying from the landlords, and it seemed too much to ask of a man to get it coming and going, at home and in the fields, from family and clueless farm owners who held us like sharecroppers in the manipulative state of cash renting. I was happy for my father, and felt bad for my slow-moving grandpa.

Inside the car we were quiet. The entire drive to pick up our fixed car was as soundless as a dream. Our grandparents slept and we did too, waking every so often as we bounced over a seam in the road or a semi roared by. At the repair station we switched cars and told our aunt and uncle good-bye, then my mother did cry, her mascara smearing onto the cream lapel of Aunt Jean's jacket. The two sisters exchanged makeup that way; my mother's cheek was smattered with Aunt Jean's pink lipstick kisses. It would be the last we would really see of that side of the family. A year later, after my mother's parents died, the kin in Terre Haute was severed from us like a bad farming accident. We couldn't feel them anymore. We'd lost them. The stumps it left us with were not from a finger or hand or leg; it was our hearts that'd become phantom, healed over time, but tingling with the medicinal effects of memory.

Finally, with Derrick behind the wheel, we were on our way back to the farm in Wabash. We all dozed again, including my mother, while our grandparents slept for almost the entire trip home. It was late afternoon, the sun bright in the sky, and I couldn't sleep as Derrick drove us past old homesteads off the interstate, where only an old barn still sagged into the weedy ground around it, the skeleton of a farmhouse in front, an open mailbox leaning toward the ground. We drove by so many of them I thought we were traveling in a circle. They looked like Old West ghost towns, deserted and lonely, from a time so long ago the silos had to be added to stage a modern effect.

At a crossroads, where we turned toward a town called Sway-zee, a farm not so broken down as the ones off the interstate stood at the edge of a ravine. It had a bright orange sign in the yard that read: Foreclosed. I didn't know what it meant, but I could see its implications in the empty sheds and abandoned tractors, in the rusty combine sinking up to its tires in a mud hole, weeds growing from the wheel wells. In a pasture next to the house, a bony herd of cattle moved stupidly from one little patch of grass to another, lost and blandly chewing their dry, wasted cud. The sight made my heart sink. I watched as Derrick deliberately turned his head in the other direction, too frightened to look at our future, the nape of his neck covered in chill bumps. In the car my grandfather woke up and looked directly at me as Derrick turned onto Highway 13 for the last twenty-five miles of the drive into Wabash. The old man fixed his eyeglasses and smiled. He winked at me and whispered something I couldn't hear. I was scared; it would take some getting used to, this new grandpa, with his odd behavior and playfulness, so unlike the man he'd been before. I stared back at him, trying to get accustomed to this new person sitting right next to me.

He leaned closer and whispered into my ear, his mouth brushing my cheek, "Wabash is the city of electric light." He reclined back in the seat, took a deep breath, and went to sleep again. If he could remember that, I thought, he might not be as different as we'd first imagined.

When we turned onto Pike Street I reached forward to touch my brother's back. He smiled in the rearview mirror, a weak, tired grin that came and went quickly. My mother sensed we were turning into the lane of the farm and she woke up. "My goodness," she said, "your mother just dreamed about the weirdest things. She did. She sure did." She was back, our third-person mother, and so were we. Darren and my dad came out of the house with their jeans tucked into gumboots. I could barely wait to see the runts as Darren opened my door.

PART III

Colored Glass
23

We plodded along the fallow field, my changed grandpa, my mother, and myself, those imaginary *rooks* (that was what I'd read in my dictionary blackbirds could be called, rooks, like crooks) in a chattering flock, perched in a row of leafy trees, eyeing me, planning on how they might swoop down and steal my fingertips when I wasn't looking. To go to the dump I had to wear two Wonder Bread bags over my hand. Early morning light pelted us through the high ceiling of dense summer leaves and tangled vines dropping down from limbs nearly as big around as some cars. A scent of wet earth and rusted cans sprang forth from the heap. It had rained for several days straight while we were gone, and the furrows and waterways held stagnant rain, algae already clinging to the surface, and the throaty sounds of bullfrogs bellowing.

On top of the heap, Grandpa Fred stood like he'd just taken the beach in Normandy. He hadn't fought in any of the wars, but after returning from Terre Haute he was convinced he'd spent time as an enlisted man, saluting everything from the boars to tree stumps as he walked the farm, a new favorite pastime of his. My mother sang in her dulcet voice, the morning breeze lifting the tune upward until it sounded as if it were being broadcast from somewhere in the middle of the towering oaks and river syca-mores. The dump, along with an adjacent ravine, had been used by a hundred cash renters before us to discard everything from medicine bottles to outdated farm equipment. There was a whole car in the center of the mess, and rolls of rusty wire, busted-up windows and gas tanks, old feeders and the bones of cattle and hogs dead from cholera, thrown over the edge rather than sent off on the stink wagon. It was a disaster, a large fissure in the earth where junk from generations before rested on top of even older waste. We weren't digging through the ravine junkyard; for that we would've had to rappel the rocky walls. Instead, we stood off to the side of what we called the Little Grand Canyon, even though it was brimming with trash and horribly ugly, and were prepared to sift through a more manageable pile of trash that was heaped on the surface.

The dump had been one of my mother's many sudden ideas. Like the fireworks from the Fourth, they'd burst into her dark-ening mind, exploding to create light where night had been; the ideas illuminated her, making the landscape of her brain clearly visible again, even if, like the clinquant glow from the '76 cele-brations or Wabash's First Electrical Light, it would recede, bring-ing the dark back. I imagined a bicentennial without freedom or power, only deep, deep darkness, so much so the word *night* held no meaning.

It wasn't that I didn't want to go to the dump, I did, but it felt weird to turn the event into a fieldtrip. She made it sound so irresistible.

"Come on, Dougie. Go with your mother and Grandpa Fred

to the dump. She's sure you might find some old stuff to play with. She wants you to go so baaaaad!"

I brought along a wooden cane from the many we kept in a metal bin beside our ginger-colored Carhartts and rows of cracked gumboots. Our back porch held the spicy scent of laundered clothes soiled by hog manure; the more you washed the crap off, the more it seeped into the threadbare fibers of the clothing, turning spicier and more pungent with every load, not a bad smell, just an overpowering one.

With the tip of the cane, I brushed aside loose pieces of metal from old appliances and flipped over spare tires, but nothing like what my mother had promised popped out of the earth; however, she found a paradise. A few feet down the knoll where my grandfather still stood erect, surveying the area like it needed tilling, she came across another whole mound unto itself; it was a heap of glass bottles, most of them with dirt packed inside. They ranged from sienna to ocher, light blue to navy, and clear to nearly fire red. The bottles were from the 1930s and '40s, left behind by a pharmacist who'd also farmed nearby. Most were old prescription bottles, and they were strikingly beautiful. My mother diligently tapped the dirt free from each one, holding them up to the bright sunlight to catch the rays. Some of them shot color straight through to the ground at our feet. My mother said, "Like a disco ball, Dougie. See what your mother is doing?" She tilted each bottle just the right way to make the light tremble over the dirt, muted rainbows spanning a section of the trash.

Grandpa Fred stumbled down off the top of the mound and approached. He seemed taken by the tricky show my mother was producing, like a child first noticing shadow and light. He got close to my mother and put his hand in the ray of yellow she made. Grandpa Fred played in the different colors until it was time to prepare for lunch. I helped my mother load all the bottles into a plastic pail and we set off for the house, walking over the sodden field, our three sets of feet making vulgar noises in the mud. My grandfather's foot got stuck in a pocket of soaked top-soil. We were almost to the house. He pulled it out with some effort but it made the sound of a deflating balloon screeching out air: pluuuuuuzzzzthhhh. He kept walking but turned to us, face as serious as a doctor's bill, and said, "Excuse me, folks. That was rude of me." He patted his stomach. "Must've been something I ate."

After lunch I burgled muskmelon rind and sweet corncobs from the plates of my family. I'd fed the runts only with milk left-overs, but I feared they would not be able to survive without more. Darren had told me not to feed them anything but milk, but I sensed another dietary need in my little herd. He'd kept his word and fed the runts as much milk as he could steal himself, even try-ing a few times to milk one of the big sows with regular babies, but you can't do that the same way one milks a cow, trust me.

Inside the shed, I pulled the morsels out of the same bucket we'd used at the dump for the glass bottles. Peanut and the others sniffed warily at the food. I pulled my chunky Barrow pocket-knife from my jeans and began cutting the food into slices the size of peas. Peanut blindly tried to find it. She sniffed the air with her little crooked face and finally locked onto a smidgen of green-orange muskmelon rind I held before her squashed nose. Once she found it she gulped it down like it was candy. I cut off another sliver with the dull blade and let her have it. I went clock-wise, giving each runt two pieces before moving on to the next. After the second round, my little foster litter started making a familiar sound: a guttural chant, a communal grunting, the same kind the litters in the farrowing barn made when nursing at their mothers' teats. The sound filled me with glee. I fed them all that I had brought, and then gave them each three ounces of milk from the two bottles. After they all had full bellies they wanted to bed down. They snuggled into a heap near my legs as I sat on the straw-covered floor. I pulled the book from my lap and started to read. They all seemed to fall asleep at once when I read to them about the grotesques, ad-libbing at certain spots to make the point that we were all disfigured: "Mom, me, you guys, and now Grandpa Fred. Grandma Enid in Terre Haute and Ray, too."

I surveyed my little runts sprawled out next to one another, a real sense of accomplishment in me as I marveled at their full bellies. "But you guys don't know Ray. He's the guy who told your mother he's maimed."

24

Buy These

It was well past dinnertime when the man knocked on our door. I hadn't seen Joe for the several days we'd been back home, but now, with the man almost pawing at the door and Joe barking ferociously, just like in his namesake's TV show, I was certain it wasn't good news. My mother went to the door, pushed aside the stars and stripes window sheers, and peeked out. Derrick and Darren were in the fields with my dad. The girls had gone across the pasture to visit with our grandparents, leaving me alone with my mother as she tried in vain to hide the fact that she was making the final alterations on my Uncle Sam outfit. She'd stumble out of her sewing room with a mouthful of pins, cloth wrapped around her wrist, and tell me to put down the book and come model for something she claimed she was making for Darren.

"Ma'am," the man in the suit said, "I'm from World Book. Wouldn't you just love to have some of the smartest children at Southwood Elementary, perhaps the high school, too? Buy these and that could come true." He had on a houndstooth jacket and a tie my Grandpa Basil would've considered gaudy. It had pinwheels on it, like the spirals on those huge lollipops.

"Why, yes," she exclaimed, brightness filling her eyes, an idea, another foray into something that could distract her. She let the man inside the house as I sat at the dining room table reading my book and admiring the picture of Jimmy. In just a week or so, I'd worn the edges of the photo down; it peeled at the corners. I'd read only the grotesque story; I hadn't proceeded past that one and wouldn't until almost a year later. I was thinking about how to make my bed higher.

My mother told the man to please sit down. He did as he was instructed, swiping the hat from his head to expose a combover that equalled nothing I've seen to date. His part started just a half-inch above his right ear, and the long strands of thirty or so dark hairs swooped across his shiny dome, the tips touching his left ear. I was amazed. I couldn't help but stare. It kept my eyes glued to his head. My mother directed her attention to me, trying to help me stop being so rude.

"Your mother sure would like for this man to tell her about the encyclopedias, Dougie." She motioned with her head for me to unlatch my gaze and listen carefully to the pitch. The man, somewhat confused, asked, "Oh, I'm sorry, where is the lady of the house then?"

"She's right here," my mother said. "Right, Dougie? Your mother's here?" I nodded my head yes.

Afraid he'd committed some social faux pas, the man tried again. "Well, anybody can see you're perhaps an oldest child?" He hinted at the answer with his eyebrows. "I mean, surely you're old enough to make decisions, but I need to talk with the lady of the house."

"That's right. You do. Right, Dougie? Your mother is very

interested in these books. She'd just love to have a set for these kids." The man grew irritated. His bald head became greasier and his armpits showed dark wetness.

The man pulled from his briefcase an elaborate order form, a single volume; A–BE; and a pen he clicked as if about to fine us. He accepted that my mother was indeed in the house somewhere. But he'd had it with the third-person talk and was simply ready to end his day on a sale, whether that was to the sister of the lady of the house or the lady herself. He didn't seem to care anymore.

It was an easy sale. He didn't have to recite the statistics about the differences in grades received by children who had encyclopedias at home versus those who did not, but he did anyway, even when my mother took the order form from him and signed it in her loopy cursive signature before his speech had even ended. I felt joy extend up from my belly. Then the man said something I can still hear in my head today as if it were one of the gospels at my grandparents' elderly church.

"Of course, the set comes complete with a two-volume dictionary just like these." He hefted out of his deep luggage two brown-and-tan books as thick as Grandma Enid's white Bible. He let them thud onto the table for the effect. He threw the cover open, and its weight slapped the maple top. He was rushing through the sale now, and read off words starting with the letter A. His lips formed sounds I'd never heard, words so long I thought he'd choke before getting to their ends. My mother clapped her hands. He retrieved the order form from her and stood up.

"Now, everybody gets excited by the books, but I need to know you're serious. I need a down payment of thirty dollars to hold them, to get them delivered to you in a couple weeks." My mother wrote him a check and he stuffed it into a large manila folder. He tipped his hat and asked, "Is that dog dangerous out there?" He looked to me for the answer, but I couldn't speak.

"When I drove up he seemed to be fine and then when I got out he started in like he was rabid or something." He peeked out the window sheers like my mother had earlier.

"I don't see him now," he said and he left at a quick pace, his black cases banging at his knees as he high-stepped it to his paneled station wagon, fired it up, and left down the lane, turning right onto Pike Street. I watched him until the car was out of sight, hoping for his sake he wasn't planning on trying to sell the World Books to the lair of devil worshippers holed up in the black and red houses in The Prairie. I prayed for him then, hoping selfishly if he was foolish enough to peddle his wares to them, he'd at least place our order first, so those shiny bound volumes would pass unto the 7 D's to use for good, looking up other words for *salesman* and *worshipper,* for *devil* and *maimed.*

As the days wore on, my central preoccupation became finding food for my runts. I'd rise earlier than everyone else and steal what I could from the pantry and dig through the trash to make certain I didn't miss any morsels that could be served to my piglets. One morning, when it was still early dawn, I packed a flashlight into a sack along with the stolen food. As I stepped off the porch with the sack full of donated goodies, I caught another glimpse of Joe's growing bloodthirst.

He was sitting in a part of the yard obscured by low limbs and tall grass, under a pear tree my mother had planted and to our amazement gave us fruit. In his mouth, another creature squirmed. I was instantly mad, and picked up a rock and heaved it at him with all my might. I missed horribly, of course, my left hand still not all that useful.

I bent and plucked a bigger rock from the wet ground. It was the size of a billiard ball. I slung it toward Joe with the intensity of guerrilla fighter. It smacked him on his side and he let out a noise like a blend between a blubbering cry and the sharp trill of a hog's squeal. He dropped the writhing creature from his mouth and growled at me from under the pear tree, the fur on his neck standing up like static on our hairy arms. He barked, grabbed the animal in his mouth, and ran off toward the back of the farm. He vanished into the high corn, the razor-sharp leaves closing behind him like jail bars. I picked up my satchel of food and walked to the shed. Joe's behavior unsettled me, made me jumpy, a word used to describe my mother's mental state. *She'll be jumpy for a while,* the doctors had said.

I opened the gate and went into the stall, but before I could get settled down in the straw with my book and treats, I heard a noise in the adjacent pen that Darren had also cleaned up when he first saved the runts for me. I hadn't noticed at first, but it had new straw in it and a gate just like the one that kept my runts from running about the whole inside of the dark barn. I placed the sack of food on top of an empty fifty-gallon oil drum and cautiously approached the other stall.

Inside, there was no heating lamp or light bulb like in the other, but I could definitely tell something was there. I peered over the gate and saw two strange figures swaying back and forth. I immediately thought of the devil worshippers again; a little trickle of pee eased into my shorts. I'd planned on whizzing in the corner of the shed so as not to wake anybody up with a flush inside the house, but now, fear in my mid-section, some urine made its way down my chunky thigh.

The two shapes came forward. I stood back and decided to go and get the flashlight from the bag. As I came back to the stall, the flashlight held out in front of me like a laser, thinking somehow it would help me combat whatever was lurking in the darkness, a rustling noise came from inside. I got up the nerve to ambush the doorway. I climbed onto the gate and shined the light into the space. Two sets of reddish eyes glared back at me. I thought number two was going to show up in my pants as well. Somehow, though, I was able to absorb what was staring back at me. The two figures began oinking and moving toward me in the familiar way I'd seen my little humpbacked runts move, a kind of labored strut. These were full-grown runts, if that's not a contradiction in terms. The pair was no bigger than spaniels, with furry hair and short legs. One had crossed eyes like Peanut, and the other one dragged its left back leg like a trapped piece of brush. It scraped at the cement under the straw. They both had warts, like ball peens poking out of their hides, covering them generously, so that touching them felt like fingering giant Braille. I was instantly excited. These runts had made it past being piglets, and they seemed successful at managing their lives, but where had they come from? I could only suspect Darren had something to do with it.

I carefully unlatched the gate and let the new runts come out. By now the other tiny runts were squealing for me to feed them. The bigger runts went immediately to the sack on top of the oil barrel and turned their snouts up to sniff. I edged around them and pulled out some rinds. The way they shared it made me laugh, each nibbling on an end until they met in the center, no squawking or fighting over the middle, like lovers eating a strand of spaghetti. When they touched their snouts together, the rind eaten, I noticed that they were a couple, mates. They were exactly the same size, shaggy and white. I thought they might be feral runts, born in the pasture and surely on the road to doom, but somehow living past their expectancy, roaming the woods, making do on walnuts and grass. Later, Darren told me I was correct. He'd found them foraging behind the barn and coaxed them into my shanty with one ear of corn on a long piece of bailing wire. With the adult couple grunting softly at my legs, I decided I had a new family and wanted them all to be together. A feeling of contentment welled over me.

For the first time I let the baby runts out into the center of the shed as well. They immediately began following the adult runts around; by simple happenstance, I'd transferred my maternal role to the couple. I fed them all the milk from the bottles and issued out all the scraps of food. I put all the runts together in the first stall and latched the gate. As if born to them, the runt piglets slept between the adults. The female, who I quickly named Enid, rolled over onto her side, and I noticed something that produced in me such glee I thought Pig Boy would shoot straight through the roof and launch into orbit over the city of Wabash, joyous light trailing from my rear. The little gilt was pregnant. Her teats, which when she'd been standing could not be seen because of her shaggy coat, like fringe dangling from a lampshade, were puffy. I'd picked up from my brothers how to tell when a sow was with babies, and she had all the telltale signs. Her belly was distended, and her four meager nipples swelled. I watched the little runts try to nurse from her and, like any good mother, she turned upright again to protect what she instinctively knew she'd need for her own coming babies. She wasn't mean about it; she sniffed and talked to the little runts as she used her nose to push a piece of rind in their direction. I watched until my eyes hurt and my hand started banging out pulses to remind me of an impending soak. When I left, the runts were all asleep again and I felt as if the building held all the love in the world. Outside the air was humid, birds slashing across the steaming pasture. Off in the distance, Joe howled, called to the half-moon still visible in the late morning sky. He sounded like he wanted something so badly it hurt.

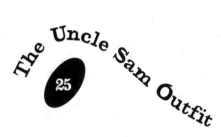

The Uncle Sam Outfit
25

The next morning my mother woke me up early. "Get up, Dougie. Your mother's going to get your grandpa. We're going back to the dump." She beamed a smile wide as a plate. She'd been working on another room, and she took me by my hand, led me to the spare bedroom, and opened the door. I was still half asleep and terribly hungry. She announced, "Lookie, Dougie!" The room was red, white, and blue (what else) with more of the glitter from the bathroom. A full-wall mural of the flag spread across one end of the room while an oddly shaped eagle had been stenciled on the other. Its feathers were painted midnight black; its claws, holding a coiling white snake, were gold. It was impressive, overwrought, and completely without comparison in my mind. I thought, if she turned this in at my school as an art project she would get super-super-extra credit, passing from the third grade right into the high schoolers' fancy art class where they made abstract sculptures from plaster of Paris molded in the small milk cartons from the lunch room.

The sun hadn't been up long when we got to the dump again. Grandpa Fred was feeling silly. He talked about how he'd once wrestled a bear just to vote in the presidential elections during the Depression while living in Detroit in a boarding house, right before he'd met my grandmother. It was all true, except the bear part. He'd always taken voting and politics as seriously as he'd contemplated the livestock and fields. When my grandparents had met in Detroit, the old woman who ran the boarding house had been feeding her tenants very thick, very fatty peanut butter sandwiches. The only thing my grandmother ever mentioned from her past was that peanut butter. My grandpa had been lanky all his life, except while living at the boarding house. My Grandma Rose would say, "I couldn't see Fred's eyes when he lived there. He weighed over 200 pounds." His normal weight was about 150.

Now, scrounging through the dump, I started to grasp how his mind had changed. He said, "I didn't think that bear was gonna let me vote. No, siree." He laughed out loud, a long whinny that took his breath away. He sucked in more warm air and carried on. "Thing was, he weighed over 200 pounds, that bear. He got that way from eating peanut butter." His stories continued on like that, mixing two parts memory with one part misapplication. It was fascinating, often hilarious, sometimes sad. He'd pick grapes in the nude, drive phantom herds of cattle in his long johns while sitting stationary at the kitchen table, and recite stories from the slivers of his nascent memory as lucidly as the country singers on the RCA turntable. One thing he didn't lose was his ability to drive. He'd always loved driving, whether tractor or truck, car or lawnmower; the man could maneuver anything with wheels.

As we stood ankle deep in the muck of the trash heap, my grandfather squinted at me through his black-rimmed glasses. He smirked and said, "I think I better get you to drivin'." He measured my height by scooting up behind me so we stood back to back. He turned me around and said, "Yep, that boy needs to be getting around." My mother kept pawing through the shrapnel of pretty colored glass. He called out to her. "Hey, lady, don't you think this gentleman here could better himself with drivin'?" She shrugged her shoulders. "Uh-huh."

"It's settled, then." He held out his hand for me to shake, and we pumped like grown men at the grain elevator betting on Knight's Hoosiers versus Keady's Boilermakers. I reveled in his newness, and even started to feel a deeper connection to him as he winked at me and turned away, stumbling over the junk to search for glass with my mother.

That night, at the evening soak, Darren read to me for the first time since we'd returned from Terre Haute. Secretly, my hand had been hurting so much I'd sometimes bite my tongue to prove something else could hurt, too. The infection that had first shown itself to my cousins continued, washed away in the Epsom but returning at the next soak. While there had been a little spotting on the gauze, an ugly yellow tinged with green, it had not gotten better or worse, but now, as Darren read and unwrapped my hand at the same time, I could feel it start to ooze, hot, from my middle finger.

The meringue ridge was broader now, and thicker. When Darren tried not to show too much concern, I knew something was wrong. I turned my head away and looked out the kitchen window to my shanty in the distance, cloaked in a brown shadow. He paused in his reading as he inspected the finger in the water, his voice cracking from puberty and trepidation. I listened closely to the words. He was reading from the book he'd given me, and, at my request, had started again on the grotesques story. I could feel my heartbeat in the water; it pulsed out a message that reverberated in the plastic tray and sent subtle shock waves up my arm to my dizzy head.

"Hey," Darren said, not reading anymore. "Look at me." His voice was soft and careful around the edges. I turned to face him, tears in my eyes, scared as a runt. He put the book down on the table.

"I'm gonna go get some peroxide, OK?" His reddish hair glistened like wet redwood in the flickering fluorescent light. I smiled, chin quivering, lips sputtering. I tried to hold it in, but the force of my fear made my dumpling throat ache sorely. As I wept I remembered the year before when I cut my leg with a scythe while chopping volunteer corn (seeds from the year before that came up unexpectedly, so they sort of volunteer) in a field of blooming soybeans next to the house. I'd sat down and hooked the sharp blade around the base of a beefy eight-foot-high stalk of green corn. I pulled hard but couldn't get it to budge. I began yanking at it with the sharp blade, and on the last exhausted pull the scythe slipped through the tendons of the corn and slammed into my leg, sticking there. I couldn't scream, but it hurt horribly; the tip had hit bone. While the gash was small, it was deep, and I begged my brother not to tell so I wouldn't have to go to the hospital and cost my parents money they were saving for the farm.

Darren acquiesced and hid it from them, vowing to go to the drugstore in Wabash and buy some butterflies for my leg. I thought he was playing with me, talking nonsense to get me to calm down. How could butterflies help my leg? I pictured giant swallowtails, their large wings camouflaged in shades of army green, landing on my deep gash and fluttering there as if taking pollen from a bloom; or a Harvester, with its gossamer wings, peach background and cinnamon dots like dripped paint, quivering above the wound, the air from its beautiful wings sucking the gash shut, healing it with sheer loveliness.

Darren left the kitchen and returned with the brown bottle. He brushed my sweaty bangs off my forehead and waited for me to lift my dripping hand from the water. Steam rose from the torn flesh. My fingers felt as if they were gone. He poured the peroxide over my hand and the fizz sounded like sizzling bacon. I closed my eyes and focused on the darkness, the ghostly outlines of amoebas drifting past my lids.

For over an hour he kept at it, pouring and dabbing, rinsing the fingers and soaking them in the Epsom again. It was getting late and I was sleepy. My body was morphing into lead. I didn't care if my hand ever worked again. Darren picked me up and with some effort started up the stairs to put me in bed. He didn't whisper when he told me about my butt. "You know, they grafted skin from your rear onto your finger. When school starts, and any kids give you heck about them, just flip them your wicked bird and tell them to kiss your ass." The ass skin was news to me. But as he toted me up the carpeted stairs, I couldn't do anything but giggle. Sleep took me into the night and toward wicked dreams, while downstairs I could hear my mother's sewing machine clacking away, and Johnny Cash singing about a blue train.

In the morning my hand felt lighter. It still hurt but something in it felt odd, almost surreal, as if it were wooden and I was all plastic, out of place and incongruent. I pulled on my clothes and work boots. The house was quiet and a broad band of warm sunlight slashed in through the narrow windows. I could smell that breakfast had been made, and the stillness told me there'd been an early rising for a specific task. Knowing that the others were hard at work made me feel I needed to take more charge of my healing. I filled the tray with steaming water myself and poured in way too much Epsom, but I proceeded to cut off the gauze and soak my hand all on my own. I read aloud to myself in Darren's voice, trying to sound smart and in control.

I now knew some of the words I'd skipped over earlier, and I took the opportunity to really enunciate them clearly when they popped up in the text, like stones unearthed while plowing—one hefty rock could rip the shear right off, leave us missing something important.

I applied the offensive-smelling salve and cut new gauze and strips of surgical tape. The tape hung in very long strips off the counter. I wrapped my hand back up, but the bandaging was loose because I couldn't get my left hand and teeth to work in tandem. It felt like an oversized glove, slack and about to slip off. I bagged my hand at the kitchen sink and tightened the twisties with extra care. I felt proud. I walked to the trash can and fished out scraps of toast and orange rinds. I dumped it all into a bag. In the refrigerator, I ripped off a whole half-gallon of milk. I warmed it on the stove and poured it back into the container, planning to fill the bottles later in the shed. I bent down and flopped the bag over my shoulder and was prepared to leave when my mother came into the kitchen holding up the piece of clothing I'd heard about, dreaded wearing, and now could see hovering toward me like a haunted spirit. I couldn't see my mother's face. She held the jumper up in front of her, totally obstructing my view of her.

From behind the suit she asked, "Well, what do you think, Dougie? Didn't your mother make a wonderful parade outfit?" Her rhetorical question sent me into wonderment, trying again to determine if there was another woman she was in contact with who was my real mother, giving her updates and asking her to ask me questions.

"Who's my mother?" I responded. She lowered the jumpsuit slowly; her dark curls appeared first, then her forehead, followed by her brown, tired eyes and broad nose, next her red lips came into focus, and finally her chin, rucked by a pout. She answered, "Your mother's your mother, Dougie. You know that." She didn't let my question stop her, though. She held the Uncle Sam suit up to me to make sure it fit. It did, unfortunately. The jumpsuit came replete with a large white plastic buckle on a belt of the same candy-striped material; after all, what's a jumpsuit without the unneeded cinching belt? She told me to strip down to my underwear to try the thing on. I did as she asked and stood in my white briefs, satchel full of runt food at my feet, as I lifted first one leg, then the other. The first uncomfortable aspect I detected was at my backside. My butt was big for a kid. It took pants designed for stocky men to accommodate its fullness, leaving my pant legs way too long, hemmed to the knee. The jumpsuit rode up my crack severely. It alienated my cheeks, defining them as two things, not one. I thought of the commercials for Playtex brassieres, the ones that embarrassed us boys when they came on the TV: *lift and separate.*

If ever a kid wanted to be someone else it was me, standing there as my mother put on her big sunglasses, as if using them for vision, and inspected me head to toe, asking me to twirl around so she could really see me good. She smiled her delight and left the room, returning shortly with a porkpie hat, cream-colored with a band of stars around the top, made out of some kind of plastic, hard as hell. She put it on my head and clapped. Derrick and Darren had been right about the getup. But I'd be lying if I said I wasn't flattered as well. She'd taken all this time to fashion it, sewing at night in her little cubbyhole, eyes bloodshot, fingers calloused, hair falling down around her face. Indeed, I must say that I willingly wore the shirts she made to school; somewhere deep inside I knew I looked silly, but what can I say, I loved them. In fourth grade she helped me make a choker necklace with a brown chain, my first-year 4-H pin in the center; a huge yellow-and-green-print polyester shirt she'd made accented it, and I had my school picture taken in it. I never saw a boy wear a choker necklace before, but she told me it looked cool, and that was all I needed.

So it shouldn't come as a surprise that I eventually came to like the jumpsuit. I didn't right then, or even before the parade, but after a few months I'd pull it out of my closet and wear it, pretending I was an Uncle Sam lookalike on the presidential campaign trail. I also wore it on a January 22, 1977, for Jimmy's inaugural ceremony.

In the kitchen she said, "Oh, Dougie, lookie," holding up a large hand mirror. "Don't you look just fine." She was teary-eyed.

"Thank you," I said, my butt cheeks numbing from their separation. A high-pitched scream cut through the humid air and into the kitchen through the open window above the sink. The house was no more than twenty-five yards from the main barn lot. It was an unmistakable cry, the wailing of a sow being rung, which meant it was having large silver staples as thick as roofing nails clamped into the pink fleshy tops of each nostril. I hated the sound; it made me feel queasy, and I could never quite accept that it was necessary. I ran out the door, leaving my mom in the kitchen with a hanky to her nose.

I snuck around the fencing to the paddock, keeping low to remain out of sight. I edged up past the old corn picker and peered around it. My brothers and father were rushing around a crate, a thin sow inside it, neck clamped, screaming with all her lungs, feet slipping in excrement as she tried to get enough traction to yank her head out of the vise. It was useless. My dad deftly clamped her nose with the rings and in a second had her released and on her way. She quietly strolled away, nose upturned, the new jewelry in her nose glinting. I stood at the edge of the lot, hidden behind the rusty implement. In my jumpsuit I looked ridiculous. When the next sow was tricked into the crate, seeing the light at the end of the tunnel and rushing for it, only to be pinched at the neck with 200 pounds per square inch in the vise, I put my hands over my ears as she cried out in pain. I'd never be able to do what the other men could. I was saddened by it, and relieved, too. My left hand shielded my left ear from the screams, but the right one hung useless, the bread bag vibrating like a reed, amplifying the sow's shrieking.

Pig Boy on the Lam

26

Two days went by and I didn't see much of my brothers, although one night during my soak Darren read a pulp novel about the sea and chests of gold drug money. He'd read to me for two months and I was mesmerized by the sound of his voice, the way he let just the right emphasis fall on just the right words. He was better at it than our library teacher when she read on a small stool and the kids sat before her on their knees, the cold hard linoleum making our bodies feel old. He was an expert reader. In my journal I started to pen some tales of my own, which were usually rehashed from bits and pieces of the books Darren read to me, and partly informed by my own imagination. I started to see the devil worshippers from The Prairie as enormous red bats, so red they were nearly black. I wrote about how they swooped down and bit off boys' fingers, their wicked cohorts, the blackbirds, the rooks, clinging to the branches of the trees near the dump. The magic potions to kill them were sealed inside pretty glass bottles, covered and wrapped by bread bags for extra protection. I used some of my Grandpa Fred's senile stories too, feeding the hero with peanut butter sandwiches that turned him into a man with bearlike strength. I tried my best to write them down, sometimes copying whole sentences from the Sherwood Anderson book.

I carried the journal with me as well. In the morning, after a soak I'd prepared by myself, my mother and grandfather again went to the dump in search of colored glass. I'd begun to love the trips. This time we didn't walk. My grandpa pulled his green pickup in front of the house and honked. The girls begged to come along but my mother informed them it was not ladylike to dig around in trash. They looked at her, puzzled. Dana declared, "You a woman, mommy."

With her sunglasses on her paper-white face she spoke softly. "No, she's not, baby. Your mother's not a woman anymore."

"Crap, you are too," Dana said, confident as an old codger telling a buddy how good he had it. My mother let a small grin take the corner of her mouth. She pulled me by the arm and we walked to the door. Grandpa Fred was in the truck, his shirt off for some reason, tapping out tiny toots with the horn. "We'll be back soon," my mom hollered back at the girls.

In the truck my grandfather asked, "You all get that Morse code I was doin?" We didn't answer as he put the truck in drive, the big black shifter in the center of the floorboard like a tree limb sprouting up from underneath the truck.

"I was telling you all it was time to go." He snorted a laugh, then patted his lap to invite me to sit. I climbed onto his bony hip, fully used to his new and improved personality. He used his bare feet to give the truck gas while I steered with just my left hand. We drove to the dump that way, the three of us: maimed, deflowered and senile, just big, ugly bills, the drain on a dream.

By the time the Canal Days Parade came around, I could drive as if I had two good hands. My grandfather wasn't able to remember to wear underwear or what his wife's name was, but he taught me to operate the pickup as if he were as clear-headed and rational as Jimmy Carter. Sometimes, when we headed to the dump in the truck, I pretended he was JC and my mother was Rosalyn. We'd bounce over the muddy holes in the bylane, the truck's tires falling into the deep recesses, splashing sepia mud up to the windows, and I'd conjure up the whole scene in my head. We were on a presidential float waving at everyone in the crowded streets, their patriotic shirts not deformed like ours, store-bought and properly fitted. It was probably that little daydream, the one I relived over and over in my head since learning to drive the truck independently, that gave me the strength I needed when my mother wheeled my bike out of the bathroom with a "Voilà!"

She'd stayed up all night again, working away like mad. I imagined her somehow magically transferring all the bicen decor from the bathroom walls right onto the bike. That's what it looked like. Exactly. She spray painted it and threw glitter on the wet paint, dousing the wheels, too: white with silver glitter, a bit of gold to celebrate the land of milk and honey, to commemorate its 200th birthday. The banana seat had been reupholstered with bright blue vinyl and the handlebars had pom-poms trailing from the ends like high school cheerleaders. It was magnificent. Had it not been for having to wear the jumpsuit and my conspicuous hand, I would've been happy to ride the thing in the parade for miles and miles.

The dictionaries from the World Book set had been delivered the night before (the rest would arrive shortly, the man told my mom, flag colors peppered all over her hair as she signed his form). Their arrival had set me to feeling overly positive about my capabilities. If I couldn't get out of wearing the jumpsuit, I'd take control of some part of the day and help out Jimmy like I'd sworn to do in my journal back in Terre Haute.

The parade was due to start in a few hours when I snuck out of the house with a duffel bag; I thought I'd need it to carry all the Jimmy Carter campaign materials I was planning on lugging back. The distance from the farm, right outside the city limits, to downtown Wabash is about four miles one way. I hadn't devised any type of sneaky plan, nor had I thought about the truck at all, but when I stepped from the front porch down into the moist gravel the idea came to me in one steadily building thought that took hold and surged forward, leaving me tossing the duffel in the back and revving up the engine.

Out on Pike Street, I was bombarded with the sights and fears from the last ride toward town, in the loader tractor. I watched the road carefully, recalling the harsh burning in my hand the morning of the accident. A rook landed on the hood of the truck, then beside it a blackbird, and next a raven, and finally, on the steering wheel in front of my face, a crow. These were the first terms I'd looked up in the perfectly bound dictionaries. I wrote them all down, planning on using them in a story. I had to sort of stand-sit as I drove to be able to see well out of the truck. The road and several stop signs were difficult to make out, for that reason and for the flock of apparitional birds obscuring my view, more and more of them landing on the truck's hood, fluttering about in angled movements, beaks and wings askew, crowding one another. I was scared, but I wanted to get my Jimmy materials before being subjected to the parade ordeal. I turned on the windshield wipers to shoo them away, and at a stop sign tooted my horn like Grandpa Fred had done. I was within the city limits now. Had it not been for my dog standing on the sidewalk with a scarlet froth around his muzzle, I might've let the phantom birds lead me into a fiery crash.

Joe dipped his fat head as I approached him in the truck. He seemed completely unaware of his surroundings. He didn't even budge when I blared the horn at him. Somehow, long before we were informed he was deaf, my brothers and sisters knew to start mouthing words to him. As I coasted past Joe, I mouthed, "Get home, Joe!" He laughed at me with his piercing eyes, not an evil kind of laugh. He was simply amused that I was trying to speak to him. He was a good dog, possessed by a lust he had no control over, but a good old boy nonetheless. In the rearview mirror I saw him duck and run, a loud blast providing him no warning; only his sense that something was coming had made him take flight. I could see the man with a cap gun running down the sidewalk where Joe had been. I was glad to see Joe had anticipated the shot, and even gladder to see he'd escaped.

My duffel was full when I left the building where the free Jimmy Carter materials were being proffered. A woman at a mahogany desk stacked high with papers had thought it was nice that a young boy was taking an interest in politics. I saw her face as I pulled out of the parking lot. She looked as if she also saw the truck crawling with hordes of pitch-black vultures, her mouth agape, eyes wide at the sight of a boy using his blinker to indicate a left-hand turn, but taking a right instead. I ignored her and the pulsing in my hand. I drove home to look up *bloodlust* in those beautifully bound dictionaries.

Don't Go Parading My Heart Around

27

My ass fared no better in the jumpsuit this time than when I first donned the flamboyant material. My drive to town had not been detected, and I was pleased to put many of the Jimmy stickers and pins on my bike, adding to my mother's masterpiece.

When she helped me pull the sleeve over my hand, that's when I first got a good whiff of the infection. With my pudgy body getting hotter and hotter under the polyester jumpsuit, I could smell it, the scent of dirty feet. I sniffed it. I inhaled deeply; the odor stuck in my nose like glue. As gross as it may sound, it was a good smell, one that left me feeling disappointed when it faded away under a breeze wafting in through the open kitchen door.

As my mother zipped me up, I watched the bottles from the dump. A whole row of colored glass shapes sat like sentries along the kitchen windowsill. Light flickered from them. Rays of ocher and sienna jiggled on the countertops. I kept my eyes fixed on the exotic light; my pupils burned from trying to keep up with the shuddering tints. She'd taken trash and made it beautiful; in my mind, my mother was a genius. I loved art in school. I thought about how to steal her bottles like I'd been stealing food for the runts.

My mother made me stand back so she could take it all in once more. "Oh my," she sighed, "this just makes your mother so proud." She kissed me on the cheek and feathered my hair with a gigantic Goody comb; I could feel the teeth digging into my skull. She began to sniffle, a light whimper that filled the room and made her appear like Mary in the Bible in Terre Haute. She stood up and tossed the comb into the sink. It clanged and landed straight up in the drain. She went to the sink and took the comb out again, and pulled it through her curly hair as she kissed my forehead. "She loves you," my mother said, as she wheeled my bike out to the truck. We were off to the parade in Wabash, a celebration of our ancestors, who first allowed electricity to light up their lives.

The hoary clouds concocted a dreary looking overcast before the parade started, but the rain held off. A Civil War rifle signaled the start with a loud blast that echoed down Canal Street. People lined the sidewalks in tank tops and cutoff jean shorts. Sitting in lawn chairs and on the concrete curbs, they were a multitude of sweaty screamers as I rode my bike down the street with several other kids who also had their rides decked out in bicentennial hoopla. My hand hurt and I tried to pedal slowly enough to not ram the float in front of me; it was awkward and before long I tipped over, landing on my other hand to break the fall. I righted my bike and climbed back on, the jumpsuit wedging up my cheeks with a great deal of gusto. I was drenched in sweat; it rolled off me as the parade escorted itself down the street.

People on the sidelines waved and clapped, oohing and aahing when the little kids on tricycles in front stopped to stare back at the audience. One child burst into tears and abandoned his trike to run to his mother jogging supportively along the shoulder of the route.

The ride was not long. Before I knew it I was back with my mother in a parking lot behind the courthouse, the clock tower rising over our heads like an appendage fallen from heaven, the same tower that had witnessed the Brush-Carbon lightbulb some ninety years earlier. I'd won second place. The trophy was blue and silver and it made me feel proud. My sisters and I sat with my mother at the corner as another portion of the parade came down the route. A man dressed in a gorilla outfit was spooking the children. He beat his chest and jumped around like he had rabies. It scared my little sister, who crawled onto my mother's lap and hid her head. A Wabash police officer played along. He chased after the man in the monkey suit, blowing a whistle and acting as if the gorilla had violated the jaywalking ordinance. They'd obviously put a great deal of preparation into the skit, but they failed to realize their dialogue couldn't be heard from the boisterous sides of the loud street, so it ended up looking like a silent movie. Their act was over when the gorilla bit the ankle of the cop, who pretended to hand down a ticket for the offense. The gorilla ate the citation and ran off, the cop blowing his whistle again, shaking his head and fists as if truly bedeviled. Most of the kids loved it, but I was scared of the whole thing like my sister and was prepared to gouge out the gorilla's eyes with my fine new trophy if it tried to come near us.

We watched as the high school band marched down the street, pom-poms and twirling batons a-go-go, the kettledrums keeping the beat in time with the thunder rumbling over the city. A rainbow of bright flags turned the corner. The color guards from

Grissom Air Force Base, Fifth District Ladies Auxiliary of UFW, and something called the Hockett Rockets all paraded past us, turning flags counter and clockwise, the crisp fabric snapping in the air, the smell of cinnamon elephant ears and buttery popcorn floating toward us as if the combined aromas were parade entries unto themselves.

Dana had fallen asleep on my mother's lap, and Dina, like always, was busy, using plastic crochet hooks to weave multicolored fabric loops from a huge bag into a neat, square pot holder. It was the clacking of her hooks I heard when the horse-drawn class emerged before our eyes, their hoofbeats a backward, loud echo to her work. The smell of manure, the leather, and their sweet sweat made me think of Terre Haute and Grandpa Basil's horses, made me miss the family there, the cousins and the Holy Grandparents' House on the coal company grounds.

A float sponsored by the Associated Milk Producers wobbled by; the wizened old men riding along the edges looked shy and embarrassed. Next, a float named "Missouri Coon Hunters" came past, complete with a real treed raccoon and authentic baying hounds. The dogs sounded hyper and out of control. The noise woke up Dana, who immediately began crying. Many kids along the route started to cry. I did too when I saw the eyes of the scared little raccoon up on the top of the pole on the float. He looked terrified, trembling and unbalanced, as the dogs tried to climb the base of the pole, clawing wildly, fresh marks on the bark, wood flying outward, airborne, landing on the pavement where unretrieved candy still lay. I imagined the poor raccoon as one of my runts and it made me mad at the men driving the float. I looked away and directly at my mother. She smiled, a weak attempt to let us know it was OK. Dana sobbed madly until the horrible float was gone.

As if the organizers knew the coon-hunting float would terrorize the crowd, the rest of the floats to the end of the parade were benign. They eased past, ridden by pretty fair queens and their runner-ups, stuck on the centerpieces like brides on wedding cakes, the girls waving mechanically, as if wound up from underneath. I fell in love with each of them, embarrassed as they passed us, white teeth gleaming in our direction, fearing they might catch a glimpse of my rotten hand and the float would stall, their smiles erased, aghast at my disability, horking over the edge of the bedazzled float at the sight of rooks pecking away at the maggots under the bread bags. These thoughts made me feel my own forehead. I was hot. Hotter than just from the heat. I was sick, I knew it.

By the time we got home the rain was falling as if a giant valve had been opened wide, the water simply falling from the sky, downpouring sheets rather than individual raindrops. As my mother navigated the truck, trying to avoid the gushing tributaries that flooded the narrow gravel lane, she hummed a honeyed tune I recognized from the hymnals in the ratty pews of the Terre Haute church. It was as if she loved the storm. Lightning cracked the aluminum sky, fracturing the darker horizon behind the red barn, the weathervanes on top twisting madly; I imagined the strength of the rotation strong enough to lift the barn off its foundation.

The truck stopped abruptly. We could no longer see out of the windows. Thunder crashed, one round after another, flashing light, and wind bending the big tulip trees. The girls clung to me inside the truck, our mother humming louder now, the soft edge of the hymn now deadened and dull, drowned out by her fear and the flushing of water off the truck.

The door flew open and Darren's face beamed oddly from beneath a garbage bag. He was soaked anyway, his white T-shirt see-through, his small patch of chest hair like a baby tarantula under scrim. He hollered above the booming claps. "Come on! Get under these," handing each of us bags like his; it made me feel more normal, maybe everyone had to use some sort of plastic to protect themselves. I thought I might vomit. I was hot and my mouth was gluey.

We all ran to the porch under the garbage bags, the girls now giggling as the storm began to lessen. The rain slowed to a regular heavy pace. The wind let up, we all sniffed the air; it was laced with earth and leaves, the balmy scent of rain on cut grass. Delicious.

My father sat on a bucket smoking a cigarette, flicking the dusty ashes into the cuff of his jeans. He hadn't spoken when we climbed onto the steps, and it wasn't until Darren and Derrick went silent too that I saw him in the shadows of the damp portico. He took long drags off the cigarette, holding the smoke deep inside, blowing it out with the disdain of a prisoner on a fifteen-minute walkabout. He didn't look angry, just tired and hopeless, as if his heart were floating in the eddying waters running wildly along the lane and into the culvert. It was close to the truth; a good thousand dollars' worth of soybean seed was flowing into the ditch, the little pink balls (coated in fertilizer) had eroded off when the downpour commenced. All he and my brothers could do was stand and watch. Now, all of the 7 D's witnessed our future swirling into the mucky water flowing through the corrugated drainage ditch. My dad flicked his cigarette into the cool breeze that stalled in front of the porch. He said mildly, "Well, the only good thing about this here," he paused and took off his cap, rubbing his balding head in slow rhythmic circles, "is that half of that seed is Grady's." He placed his cap back on like a cowboy adjusting a Stetson, about to saddle up. He stood and looked at us all. "You think that son-of-a-bitch would believe his half washed away and ours was still in the ground?"

We didn't speak. I saw doubles of everyone, blurry images of the faces I knew like my own; they swayed and shimmied like a mirage. I swallowed hard. He let out a blast of laughter that cued the rest of us. We laughed and slapped at our knees while my mother went and pulled every strainer, colander, sieve, and sifter she could find from the mousy cabinets in the kitchen. We kept right on laughing as we walked down the lane to the culvert to place the kitchen equipment under the flowing water, rescuing our seed and bringing it to safety on the tailgate of the truck, where we poured the salvaged, cleaned jewels into a burlap sack, telling ourselves we were saving our own, while the landlord's washed into the Wabash River, and from there into the Ohio and the mighty Mississippi. The soybeans rushed through the pipe, carried along in the maple-colored water. They hit our metal catchers, plinking, some ricocheting off and landing again in the flooding waters. It was all like a dream to me, everything hazy and silver, the voices and footsteps echoing inside my dizzy head, but I didn't say anything, because at one point, when my dad tried to crack jokes about the flood and the landlord's half, I noticed his bottom lip quivering as he told my mother at the tailgate of the truck everything would be all right. It was that lip, how it shuddered in the drizzle, straining to hold back a complete bawl, his dreams washing away, that I would remember forever. I let it enter my woozy, iridescent dream. I held it there gladly, hoping I'd be able to heal it.

Poisoned Heart

23

I woke up after midnight, sweat so thick on my body that the smiley face pajamas my mother had made clung to my thighs as if I'd taken a shower in them. My head had cleared but I felt dreamier than before; my legs were light and the house felt as if it had bobbed out to sea. I climbed out of my bed and crept down the stairs, the weightlessness in my torso gliding ghostly from one step to the next. At the kitchen table my parents were trying to calculate figures. They spoke in hushed voices, their lips moving in slow motion; the pencils they each held waved back and forth across the pages of a spiral notebook.

I stood at the doorway and watched them. At the table my mother seemed as well as she'd ever been; something around her eyes suggested she was on the mend. The wildness that had twinkled deep within her pupils had calmed, and as she rubbed my father's neck, the kitchen ablaze in hues of silver and gold and bright red, white, and blue plastered over the cabinets, I thought maybe their dream might come true after all. The sheer fact that they'd mustered up enough optimism to try committing it to paper once again was enough to make me step forward and speak.

"My hand really hurts," I said, barely able to get the words out of my mouth before I lost it and slobbered and cried. At the table they cut off the bandages and unwrapped the gauze from my fingers. The smell of dirty feet was even more pronounced and the meringue ridge that I'd first excavated in Terre Haute was now taller and bubbly. A red line stretched from the center of my palm up past my wrist, a horrible asp about to strike at my heart. My mother met my dad's glance. They prepared the soaking tray, the steam filling the kitchen, Epsom salts swirling grainy in the water as my hand went in. After a few minutes something popped. I felt a huge rush of pressure exit my entire arm. A circle of mucus rimmed the edge of the tray. Heat rose in my head then, as if the infection had somehow insulated the rest of my body from its curse. The serpentine redness climbed up my forearm like a thermometer nailed to a fence post. I was aware of the danger; at the hospital they'd cautioned us about the risk that the fingers could turn on me, leave the hand fighting itself, while the white blood cells could do an about face and end up poisoning my heart. Amputation, as silly as it sounded since the fingers had already been cut off once, would be the only answer. It had terrified me all summer and now, with a vast emptiness in my arm, I wanted badly for Darren to read to me. I asked for him and my mother smiled, turning to walk purposefully up the stairs to our bedroom to wake him.

His hair wild and bushy, he forced himself to focus on the words awkwardly slipping from his mouth, struggling to get his mind to move from slumber and dreams to the act of reading, sleep in the corners of his eyes like crystals of sand. After a few sentences he got into it. He paused to explain where he was in the story, providing a synopsis that the publisher would've been proud to use for the back cover. Together we sat at the table until dawn, Darren reading and helping refill the tub with fresh water and new Epsom. We probably did ten soaks altogether, hydrogen peroxide applied every half hour, my normal fingers pruny as Grandpa Fred's cheek. By sunup my hand had been cleaned and repackaged. The amputation wouldn't be needed, but I was exhausted; so were Darren and my parents. I was under strict orders not to fool around with my runts, but a few hours later, I was given permission to visit the shed to see my one perfectly healthy piglet, born to the two adult runts. They'd conspired to give birth to a litter of one, and I wasn't going to miss seeing it on account of my dead fingers. Darren had gone out to feed them, my little secret now fully divulged to the whole family, but he tromped back inside with a simper on his face. He looked at my mother at the sink and gave her a little wink. He said, "Guess what, Dougie?" And I knew the runts had had their babies; on the way out to the shed I'd find out the plural was singular.

The little runt mother lay on her side; a teeny lone black-and-white ball of fuzz nursed from her flat belly. I was astounded at the little creature's singularity, the spectacle of its sole feeding. I crept closer, with Darren at my side to chaperone, making sure I wouldn't get carried away and infect my hand again. I crouched down next to the runt mother and whispered random words. She made effeminate grunts, rolling her one eye toward the rafters, the white sliver expressing her pure contentment. She was proud. She'd delivered into the world a gift. On most farms she and her solitary offspring would've been considered nothing more than fodder for the field, killed and tossed away to give back to the earth the only endowment a runt could hope for: fertilizer for the future corn to feed their able-bodied cousins, but here, in the shed on our cash-rented farm, I was able to witness a place for them.

I saw the newborn runt as a savior, just like in the Terre Haute Bible, a baby swaddled in straw by a manger, meek and mild and full of hope. I needed something to believe in and the runts were my salvation.

I knelt down and watched the mini-piglet nurse. It was a little boy, its tail so small it looked like string. With my good hand I stroked his fine, humped back. It had been a long night, and we were tired, but for the next hour or so my brother and I talked about how we could fix up the shed to accommodate even more runts. I made lists of needed items in my journal as Darren droned on about appropriate husbandry practices and the corn-to-pig ratio. He estimated the ages of all the other runts and when they could be expected to successfully mate. On and on the conversation went until, that is, he arrived at our fork in the road.

"If we keep it up, we could make enough money by selling them to buy real pigs to breed." As soon as he said it, he knew he'd made a mistake. While I accepted some of the realities of the farrowing house, I'd ignored that those same principles had anything to do with my family of runts. He tried to gloss over it by quickly telling me about how we would need to get our own vials of medicine, vitamin pellets, syringes, and a substantial stash of fresh straw. He even talked about how we could cut a hole in the back of the shed and fence in an area outside for grazing, but none of it distracted me. We were different from one another, all of us were, and that was normal, but first discovering it for myself I felt like I was in exile. I believed my runts were real pigs, even greater; they were perfect angels sent to me as a sign. Darren was pragmatic and I was a dreamer; he could be president while I could only write copy about the inherent goodness of his campaign. I'd thought I was more like Jimmy, but I discovered it was actually my brother who could manage a farm and find the time to run for office, doing both things with equal sincerity. In just a couple months, after we went back to school, I'd see him don the blue and gold corduroy FFA jacket to hold office in our local chapter, his full name in cursive stitches above the left breast. He wore that jacket like Patton, his back so straight one might think a board had been inserted for show. He'd show up in the *Wabash Plain Dealer* too, a whole news story on how he and a few cohorts were going around to the city schools teaching kids what all went into their beloved cheeseburgers: cows' milk as cheese, beef, wheat for the buns, produce in the tomatoes, pickles, and lettuce.... He fielded questions from the class and I knew someday I'd be writing speeches for his campaign, the maimed brother in the background, just like Billy Carter.

Once our jabbering was through and the shed was still and quiet, all the runts asleep, we could hear Joe barking like mad in the distance. Darren asked, "That show's not on anymore, is it?" It was a question in the form of an apology, his trying to smooth over our unearthed differences. I didn't answer him, but I could feel something shift inside me; I grew up a little. Too, I accepted how different my fingers would someday look. I admired both of Darren's hands as we walked out of the shed, the skin over his scraped knuckles prettier than if they'd been completely unharmed.

Ear Envy

29

A few days later, the nail on my finger fell off. Joe came to the back door, whimpering. It was about to storm outside. My mother was filling the plastic tray with warm water and Epsom salts; I was down to one soak a day now. Darren and the rest of my brothers and sisters were out back taking down jeans and white underwear of all sizes from the clothesline. Black thunderheads roiled above the red barns, and sporadic raindrops hit the ground like firecrackers, smacking hard dirt, jumping in the dust.

I got up from the kitchen table and went to see what was wrong with Joe. The rain picked up and the sky went so dark it seemed as though I was up past my bedtime. My brothers and sisters, all soaked, rushed by me into the house, clutching armloads of damp laundry. Joe stayed near the end of the porch, not making any sound now, but licking his chops and panting heavily. As I got closer, I could see pink foam around his muzzle; it splatted onto the concrete and over his paws, which held something wiggling, to the porch. He eyed me carefully, occasionally pausing to bite and pull at the thing squirming under his heavy paw. I felt tears begin to well up. A few blackbirds cawed behind me, threatening to dive down and peck off what was left of my nasty finger. Joe began to growl, the nape of his bristly neck surging with every step I took. As much as we'd tried to ignore it, we'd all felt something awful and mean in him, just underneath his shiny coat and muscular frame. I was ready to face what I'd suspected about him: that he had become bloodthirsty.

I stopped when the end of my work boot was just an inch from Joe's front paw. He glowered up at me. The storm began to toss raggedy lawn chairs across the backyard. Joe snarled, teeth bared, his eyes fixed on a point to the left of my head. I felt hate surge in my chest, as I could now clearly make out what he had pinned to the cold porch: a baby pig, no more than a few days old, its fuzzy head sticking out from beneath Joe's paw, not one of my runts, but a pig from the farrowing house.

I was scared of course, but perhaps too stupid to realize that Joe might actually bite me. Or maybe I simply didn't care at that point. The little pig, white with black spots, made a horrible gurgling cry. Joe snapped at my good hand as I reached down to take the piglet from him. Determined, I tried again, plucking the little thing away as Joe turned to leave the porch.

By now I was crying and talking out loud to myself. I didn't want to look down at the piglet, which felt only mildly warm and barely alive in my hand. When I surveyed it for injuries, I noticed right away that its little ears were gone, chewed down to nothing more than tiny flanges of rose. My mother and the other kids were folding clothes in the laundry room as I carried the piglet to the steaming basin of Epsom salts. Slowly, I dipped the little pig's feet into the warm water. His bony sides strained to rise and fall, and he moved his head a bit as I dangled his soft hooves into the salt solution, blood oozing like jelly from the holes in his skull. His eyes were closed, long lashes matted and still. With a weak cough of blood, the piglet went limp, his lungs no longer pushing under fishbone ribs.

Still, I kept washing him in the water, taking care to cleanse Joe's thick slobber from his nostrils, dabbing at the blood around his head. I tucked the piglet into a kitchen towel and cradled him like a doll. I said a prayer for the tiny creature and sat in the chair studying his altered head. Though I was sad to the bone, I needed to understand what I was seeing. Ears make a pig's face; without them they appear alien. But there is also something regal about an earless pig, a kind of ancient, distorted beauty perhaps understood by tribes that practiced head shaping. (I'd learned about them in social studies.) I stroked his wounds, trying to make sure he knew he was kingly, and that I would put him to rest.

Behind me a door opened. I quickly grabbed the piglet, stuffed him and the towel under my shirt, and darted out the door. Outside, I looked around for Joe, but he was nowhere in sight. The storm had blown over; the sun shone above the barns like aluminum. Swifts and barn swallows dipped about the towering weathervanes on the cupola, using their radar to pick off wet, slow-moving insects for dinner. A row of blackbirds sat on the white barn lot fence, staring at me as I carried the piglet papoose-style to the garden. I collapsed to my knees and began pawing at the ground with my good hand near a tepee of snap peas. I placed the piglet in the hole I'd made, towel over his body like a shroud, and used my muddy hand to cover him. Then I scrambled to my feet and rolled an old car tire from a nearby shed and put it over the grave.

Back in the house, I discovered that the dirt and blood and dog spit my mother found in the tray of Epsom salts had worried her. She thought I'd gotten my fingers dirty during the day, causing them to bleed again, and Joe's slaver looked a lot like the beginnings of another infection. She quizzed me about it, but I only shrugged my shoulders and sat silent at the kitchen table, the steam of the newly filled tray forming a haze about our faces as Darren read to me. My mother used a double shot of salts to rid me of whatever trauma I was not talking about. Perhaps trying to get me to talk, Darren stopped reading and asked if I had a story of my own to tell. I nodded my head yes.

"It's called 'Pig,'" I said.

My mother smiled at the title, and I realized she was listening. She must have been glad I'd finally started to tell wholesome farm tales rather than the crime-novel imitations I'd been spinning during other soaks.

"There's this pig with no ears," I began.

The smile on my mother's face drifted away, and she went into the pantry and began shuffling the boxes and cans around. Darren told me to go on. I felt shaky. My throat tightened.

"This pig with no ears is a killer. He's got two big, bloody holes in his head, and he's full of rabies. He goes around trying to eat people." My voice started to quaver. Darren put down his book. I felt the hard ridge of a nascent sob in my throat. "These black-birds have been sitting on his snout and picking meat from the holes in his head."

I broke down crying. My mother, getting a little better each day, shot out of the pantry to console me as Darren lightly lifted my hand from the water, softly patting it with a towel. They put me to bed early while my other brothers and sisters asked what was wrong with me. Eavesdropping from the dark bedroom upstairs, I heard my mother say, "Your brother's just trying to get used to his fingers."

Very early the next morning, a farmer named Higgly came knocking on our door. My father went out on the porch to talk with him. For a long time all my dad did was nod his head in agreement. I'd woken up feeling better that morning and had been anxious to get back to the piglet's grave to make sure nothing had dug him up, but now, as I watched the conversation on the porch, I knew it was bad news about Joe. I ran back upstairs. From the window directly above the porch I could see into the bed of Mr. Higgly's pickup. There, sprawled out as if ready for a formal funeral viewing, was a large sow, her ears gone, a crimson crown of thick blood about her head. The rest of her was white as flour.

I went to the closet and fumbled with one hand to put on my overalls. From downstairs, I heard the kitchen door open and my father calling us to come to the table. I snuck behind the school clothes hanging in the closet and stood there silently as my father called my name. Slowly, I parted the clothes and tiptoed down the stairs, giving myself the option to sneak back up undetected if I needed to.

My dad laid it all out for us, what we were going to do. He told us we could be fined, or worse, brought up on charges if we didn't take care of Joe. He said Mr. Higgly was asking for three hundred dollars for his lost sow. Mr. Higgly, we were told, was a reasonable man, and he had a brother-in-law who worked at Grissom Air Force Base, not twenty minutes from us. They trained drug-sniffing dogs there, our father said, and they were always on the lookout for purebred German shepherds. It was decided: the next day we would all drive Joe to Grissom together, sort of a sad and morose family outing. Joe didn't seem crazed or thirsty for more blood as my dad tied him to a tractor in the front yard for his last night with us, just trying his best to look proper and fit for keeping as he lay down quietly by the front tires, his ears slicked back, the smile gone from his face.

We arrived at Grissom in our brown GMC station wagon. A state trooper with a large mustache and hair like a sink brush escorted us into a barren white room. We waited as he took Joe to a fenced-in run behind the building. My father signed some documents, handed over Joe's purebred papers, and returned to sit with us. My mother filed the girls' nails while my brothers circled the room, looking at things that were not there.

A door opened behind us. It was well concealed: white hinges, a white doorknob, too. A man in a dark green military uniform brought in a fine-looking dog that could have been Joe's twin were it not for the different markings on its muzzle. The state trooper came back and addressed our family as if we were a high school class.

"This is a small marijuana cigarette," he said, holding up a plastic sandwich bag. He looked directly at me. "Son, come up here."

I didn't want to go, but my father nudged me. I scuffled toward the trooper.

"You ever gonna smoke, son?" he asked.

I shook my head no, holding my injured hand behind my back.

"What's that?" he asked, cupping his furry ear.

"No," I said lightly.

My mother smiled at the other kids.

The trooper got down on one knee and spoke into my face. "Now, son, I'm going to put this in your shirt pocket." He paused to wave the military man and the dog out of the room. Then he stuffed the dope into my pocket. "Now I want you to just sit over there with the rest of your family, and when Corporal Stanely and Butch come back in here, he'll find it before I count to five." He stood back up. "OK?"

I nodded my head and went back to my seat.

Butch came back in with his ears pricked and his tail erect. His eyes shone with a lucid intensity, as if, while outside the white door, the military man had fed him some drugs for a boost. The state trooper stood back and smiled impishly while Butch sniffed the concrete floor around my siblings' feet, steadily filing down the row past my mother and father to me. The trooper was counting out loud. Before he reached three, the dog started to go straight for my pocket, but then he changed directions, rooting and snorting with immense suction at my side. Scared, I moved forward in my chair, exposing my bandaged fingers, the object of his mad sniffing.

The state trooper began to yell at the dog. "Butch! Heel, Butch!"

The dog got his teeth into the bulky gauze and began to pull gently. I thought he was going to eat what was left of my fingers. I started to shiver. I was so different, even animals could detect it.

My father stood up and tried to get the state trooper to call off the demonstration. "OK," my dad said, "let's get this over with."

Butch's handler came and retrieved him, and the dog was out the white door before I could even put the tape back around the wad of gauze. Disgusted, the state trooper stomped toward me, heavy boots thudding the floor, and pulled the dope from my pocket. He turned to leave, but then paused to address my parents, his back to us.

"We'll evaluate your canine and call you with the results. If he's found suitable, you'll be compensated." He strode through the white door and disappeared.

A week later we got a call during dinner. My father hemmed and hawed on the phone. Then he walked quietly to the table where, for once, since the accident and my mother's hysterectomy, we were all sitting down together to eat.

"That was the people at the air force base," my father said. He surveyed us around the table, his flannelled chest rising rhythmically. "Joe is deaf."

For a moment, no one spoke. My dad said again, "The dog is deaf; it can't hear." He scratched the top of his head, clearly trying to absorb the news himself. Finally, he went to his chair at the end of the table and sat down. "They can't use him."

We ate in silence, the noises of the meal more apparent than usual: the clang of a pan lid, the chirp of a glass hitting a dinner plate, the scrape of a spoon as it caught a mouthful of peas from a bowl. I can't say any of us knew what to make of the absurd news we'd just heard, though our lives on the farm had been full of absurdity. In the truest sense, all farming is cruelly ironic: fields of green can be wiped out by too much fertilizer; hogs sometimes get spooked and eat each other the night before they're to be butchered; and farm kids get sucked into the same machinery their parents plan on handing down to them.

I sensed that something about Joe's fate would alter me for good. Here was a story. The farm and the pigs and my entire family were all stories that I could tell someday. If I practiced and read and paid attention to what I had been taught, I could use my wicked bird to write something that would heal more than my fingers.

We picked up Joe that afternoon and brought him home and tied him once again to the tractor in the yard. I bolstered the door to my runts with stacks of straw and guarded it whenever I could, sometimes sleeping out there with Darren. Over the next few weeks, Joe got loose and chewed the ears off three of our sows and a neighbor's feeble old boar before we did the awful thing we had to do. We took him to the Humane Society, where he "went to sleep," my mother told me. It was the best she could come up with, I am sure, but I knew that Joe had been killed for threatening our livelihood. That night I woke up terrified that the blackbirds were in my bed, eager to peck at me. When I opened my eyes, I thought I saw Joe's ghost at the foot of our bed. I scooted closer to Darren, where he told me the safest story he could think of, full of candy canes and presents galore.

A couple of the pigs that Joe mauled lived. And one of them, a female, had enough nipples left to be kept for birthing. For years she had strong, healthy litters of piglets of all colors. Occasionally, a city couple out on a drive would pass our pasture and catch a glimpse of this four-hundred-pound sow parting the high grass with her pointy, earless head. They'd quickly pull their car over, and Darren, quite the entrepreneur, would charge them a couple of bucks to hear the story behind the funny-looking sow.

Then he'd come and get me, my fingers completely healed now but crooked and lobster red, and usher me down the lane to where the couple stood by the fence, feeding the sow clumps of ditch grass. I'd tell them how she'd been born with no ears, but she could smell better than any animal could. She even got a job sniffing out drugs part-time for state troopers. I went into great detail about her ability to hide in the grass without detection, her head like a small boulder, invisible to the untrained eye. I spoke slowly, with a regal air, when I told them she was descended from an ancient breed of pigs that had no need for ears.

I'd pause just the right amount of time before saying, "We love her just the way she is..." The family would look up at me and Darren, standing side by side as I sealed the deal: "...even though she can't hear us telling her." I'd feel the story make me whole, my brother's perfect right hand supporting my back.

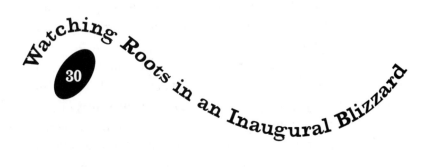

30 Watching Roots in an Inaugural Blizzard

Snow had fallen for three days straight; it piled up outside the house, insulating us from the sound of the winds, drifting the snow into expansive ridges stretching as far as our blinded eyes could see from the living room windows. School had been closed indefinitely. For the first few days, we all rushed out of our beds to each sit on a heating vent, our father's large white T-shirts pulled down over our winter-dried and scaly kneecaps, listening from every corner of the room to the voice crackling over WOWO. The man shivered into the microphone and told us that our school, along with many others, was closed, but after ten, fifteen, twenty inches had fallen and the forty-mile-per-hour winds kicked in, we just assumed the schools would be buried until spring and stayed in bed until it was time to help with the animals outside, my runts now allowed to stay in a heated part of the big barn. Jimmy Carter had been sworn in just a few days before, and I watched it with my Grandpa Fred at his house, wearing my Uncle Sam getup and him thinking it was FDR who walked down the street in the cold, waving to people, that perfect smile on his farmer's face, as we both clapped and drank coffee before the black-and-white TV.

We worked in the cold for days in the late part of January 1977, but there was another high spot, something we weren't alone in savoring.

Roots started on the twenty-third, a Monday, and aired each night for one and a half hours. For eight days it ran like that, an event we made popcorn for, and prepared whole loaves of cinnamon toast to commemorate. On average, 80 million people watched each of the last seven episodes. One hundred million viewers, almost half the country, saw the final episode. In a cover story, *Time* magazine reported that restaurant and shop owners saw profits decline while the series was on the air. The report noted that bartenders were able to keep customers only by turning the channel selector away from basketball and hockey and tuning instead to those stations carrying *Roots.* Parents named their newborns after characters in the series, especially the lead character, Kunta Kinte. We were a white trash farm family of cash renters, living dangerously on the brink of bankruptcy, yet the story rang true in our cold red ears. Of all the memories I have of that year, it's watching *Roots* with my broken-hearted family that moves me the most. It's stupid and silly, overwrought and melodramatic, but if I could take a guess at what things might run through my mind when I move from this earth and beyond, surely those eight cold nights in January 1977 will be in the top ten.

For me, a budding storyteller, Alex Haley had done something I couldn't have understood at the time, yet I sensed it: he'd loved his ancestry so much that he re-created their horrible and lovely lives, before and after tragedy, and gave it back to an indifferent America, and by doing so changed the discourse of humanity. He made his family ours, and lying under all those covers with my mom and dad and brothers and sisters, the smell of wintry air deep in our pores, Vaseline on our lips thick as honey, I wished for the day when I might give it a go myself. Sherwood Anderson's grotesques and Haley's slaves did more to char inside of me the scalded brand of a writer than anything else I can pinpoint, save for my brother's reading and my fingers having been torn off at the root.

The blizzard was brutal during the day, offering up only frigid temps and blinding walls of white as we tried to save the hogs from freezing to death, a task we managed well, including my runts, but at night, at night it was all worth it because we got to take in another family's tortuous struggle. The house seemed even warmer then. We piled blankets on top of blankets and crawled underneath the pallets with buttery fingers, shushing one another as the miniseries recapped what had happened the night before. We didn't know there was a book to go with it, but later, in junior high, it would become one of my favorite things to read over and over.

My mother would say, "Quiet down, kids, your mother..." and an invisible gear would shift in her face, backing up and changing her mind into the desired mode: first-person, singular. She'd stammer a bit, then continue. "I, I want you kids to see this. Listen now." She started shedding the third person in the late fall and while I was happy to see Your Mother take flight, I was also sad to see her go, flying away little by little, a rook on the wing, disappearing slowly but never completely fading. Even today, she still comes around, still appears on the phone to give me reports on her well-being. It's comforting to know she'll never fully go away or entirely come back. On the phone now, when she pops up, I swear I can smell her Aqua-Net hairspray, hear her sewing machine rat-at-tat-tatting out a complex pattern, and I expect her to mention something about red, white, and blue paint, maybe some glitter to boot.

Along with her healing, which would not be complete for another twenty-five years, she'd taken a job to help us survive. When we'd gone back to school months earlier, she went to work at a factory in Huntington. Our father, who was already working extra shifts at the Celotex ceiling tile factory, never seemed to tire. He worked the farm tundra with us all day and then clambered into the truck to head off for eight hours of shift work. He never slept, it seemed, except for the occasional catnap after a big lunch prepared by the girls and my mother.

One night, after Kunta Kinte cut off his foot to hurl himself into freedom, the phone rang. We'd all been sitting numbly in the living room after the TV shut off, another wave of the blizzard bearing down on the entire state. We didn't speak, just tried to absorb what we'd seen. My dad got up in his droopy long johns and went to the phone. It was a black rotary phone, the handset heavy as a horseshoe. We could hear him mumbling in the next room, then the heavy phone falling into the cradle, his double-socked feet returning. He appeared in the living room with a dour look on his face, the sideburns like flames on his cheeks. He pointed to Darren and spoke.

"You set a trap in the woods next door?" Darren seemed to already know the question. He answered quickly. "Yes, sir. I set it for a red fox. They pay thirty-five dollars for each pelt in Roann." My father didn't seem as angry as he did irritated at having to go out at night in the dreadful cold.

"Come on," he said, pointing to both of us, the other kids still snuggled under the blankets. "That was the landlord's kid. You know, the one with too much money for his own good." He wiped at his forehead as he pulled on his jeans over the long johns. "He's a nature lover and he's swearing to God he's going to have his daddy kick us off this farm for that trap." He managed to get dressed as we shot around the room putting on our own clothes.

I wasn't sure why I was going, but I didn't question it. Maybe it was because I would've begged to come along anyway; I liked to be around Darren as much as I could. But as I pulled on my snowsuit, I felt something lurking dark and ominous around the call, reminding me of Joe. My dad settled it when he said, "He's out there now, in the woods. That fox is in the trap. He's all bloody and crazed."

Darren looked half-proud and half-scared. He tucked in his shirt and pulled on a wool cap. I had one of those hats with flaps and a chinstrap; I snapped it firmly in place and followed my brother and dad to the truck. I felt an anger building inside me toward my brother. I knew he was learning all sorts of tricks and puzzles about living only from the earth; he never stopped reading about hunting and farming, growing things and curing meat and hides. I imitated him as he pored over the beautiful encyclopedias, the only real books we had in the house, but I chose sections about past presidents and playwrights who wore high-necked collars. Up until then, though, I'd thought his reading was simply a way to increase his knowledge, nothing more. I never thought he'd go from gathering the information to testing it, organizing the bits and pieces he found in print to actually come to some tangible outcome, like trapping a poor fox.

The night was colder than I can ever remember experiencing since; the sky was clear, the stars as white as the snow under our feet. The wind had backed off, and a sputtering of flurries filled the air with a delicate pruinose. Christmas had been over for nearly a month, yet this new excitement, even if it was peppered with fear, made the night seem special.

It took a long time to get to the house just across the pasture where Grandpa Fred, spiraling further and further into dementia, holed up with his wife, who he thought was his mistress. Darren had set the trap in the woods where my grandparents lived, also under the rule of our landlord. Inside the truck the heater blew like a torch. Our dad had to maneuver around cliffs of towering snow, drifts so high our neighbor's cattle walked right over the top of the six-foot fence without even knowing they were free.

The headlights swept over the barn thirty feet in front of us. If we kept on a straight course we'd end up parked inside the warm hay mow, thick native planks supporting the chassis, perhaps my father letting us take a real quick drag off a nice-smelling Salem Light, the truck idling like we had all the time in the world to sit and smoke and bullshit, but of course the truck veered off to the left and wound past the side of the barn. As we climbed the slight ridge we could see a distant light at the end of the wide-open field. The landscape in the dark was totally lunar—white and gray, full of dips and crevices. It seemed as though we might slip off the moon's surface and fall into the vast black space. I had to pee.

Our father hadn't spoken much since getting in the truck and now, as he pulled the truck up alongside a white Chevy Malibu, peace signs and beads hanging in the back window, he said, low, "Let me do the talking here. This kid wouldn't know his own shit from mud." Darren and I stayed in the bench seat as my dad stepped from the truck. He smashed his cigarette in the snow, as if there was a bona fide possibility of three feet of snow going up in flames like a dry forest.

The headlights illuminated the edge of the woods and lit up our dad's back as he lumbered toward two college-age kids standing close together. He approached the landlord's son, who wore a ratty old jean jacket with embroidery around the pockets and buckskin fringe hanging under the sleeves. Darren noticed. "That dumbass doesn't have any room to talk. He's wearing deer hide." He pointed quickly, leaving a hot spot of fog on the window where his finger touched. He wiped it away. I still had to pee.

I was about to tell Darren I was mad at him for setting the trap, but before I could muster up the guts, our dad waved us from the truck. I got out with Darren, who helped me tromp through the deep drifts toward the men. I could smell alcohol and deep-fried food when we got to them. Our dad had lit another cigarette and puffed on it between cold breaths, the smoke and exhaled air like ghost on ghost.

"Man here says you set a trap on private property without asking." He sucked in another long drag. "He's not too happy 'bout it, either." Darren's eyes were watery, from the cold, I thought. The guy's eyes were bleary from drinking and smoking pot, the smell of weed so pungent he must've been bonging in the car with his buddy just before we arrived. He started in on my brother.

"What the fuck do you think you're doing? This is our land. You people just cash rent here, you don't have any right in the first place messing with nature, let alone on ground we just let you stay on!" He seemed tired after yelling. Our dad looked like he might just eat the guy in one big swallow; instead, he nodded at the man. The guy took Darren by the arm and I followed, our dad trailing behind. We all walked into the woods, just a few feet, the boughs of the pine trees hanging low, nearly touching the ground from all the snow they held. Under a branch, in a spot barely dusted with snow, the fox lay in a mess of blood, its ultra-white teeth bared, some red on the tips, hissing at us. It reminded me of a snake, and I felt like I might vomit. The fox was small, its bushy tail flapping back and forth, nearly dead. Its back foot was caught in the brown clamp of the trap; near the hip it had gone to chewing, trying to free itself and nearly bleeding to death in the process. My memory here starts to get fuzzy. Darren says I peed my pants and cried, while he toughed it out and took the brunt of the lecture, the landlord's son hammering away at him in the cold before getting the munchies and heading off abruptly with his buddy. I remember only the sight of the poor fox, his leg nearly gnawed through, a white bone exposed, his beady, wild eyes darting, so scared his bowels had given way. I remember thinking of the black man on the *Roots* show, how he'd done the same, hacked off his own foot for a chance at freedom. I remember Darren crying too, ashamed of what he'd done, pissed off as we all were at the landlords that held us captive and kept us from our dream. I recall my father saying to the hippie, "That's enough," the words so hard and steely coming out of his mouth, I wondered how close the guy was to death himself that night. He had freedom and opportunity when he drove out of the tundra, heading to his swank bachelor pad in town, while we had more work and deferred dreams when we finally got back to the house his daddy owned and climbed into our beds. One thing does stand out, though, so vividly I question its reality. I can see my dad taking the poor little fox in his arms and placing it in the truck seat, taking the time to ease the metal trap from the crushed leg and combing the fur down on its neck, telling Darren he'd made a mistake, that nothing is as bad as feeling trapped.

The next night we watched *Roots* as we had been, cooking hot food and preparing the living room to stay warm. My mother had stapled plastic over the windows, a thick sheath to keep the wind from gushing through the cracks. With the windows sealed the room was even warmer. We all climbed under the covers, smelling like Ivory soap, windburnt faces aglow, the 7 D's settled down for a show. It would've been impossible for us to know our future, of course, lying under the warmth, munching popcorn. We couldn't have known that we would get our farm in just four years, even after Grandpa Fred got worse and worse, needing full-time care for the Alzheimer's he'd be diagnosed with. Or that Dina would need an expensive operation for the scoliosis the nurse at school would find during a PE physical. In defiance she entered her own X-rays in the school science fair as an exhibit. The ugly, evil medical bills from all of our bodies wore on my father like sandpaper, grating him to the bone week after week. We couldn't have known my mother would spiral into depression once again from her hysterectomy. Even if we had known, it still would've been ruined. After we saw the dream come true, it would just as quickly disappear in a deluge of falling prices and natural disasters. Too much rain, then not enough; broken axles and bad markets; stolen equipment and children beginning to dream of their own futures, off the farm, free to go anywhere. In 1985 the farm we did buy would be taken from us, foreclosed, and all the equipment sold off, my dad's parents in a Medicare nursing home, and our family broken up. But we didn't know that on the night of January 30, 1977. All we knew was we were warm and together, the final night of *Roots* narrating our own past, giving us hope for a kinder future. Under the blankets our dad passed a loud round of gas during the commercials; it made our mother put a pillow over her face. We all laughed so hard it felt like we'd explode. He said, "There goes that little mouse on a motorcycle, kids," and then we were quiet, holding our bellies, not able to breathe, as the music started and we watched the TV until it was over.

I hate to fly, can't stand it. I've gotten a prescription for Valium in the past, but I just really didn't feel right taking it this time, with my nine-year-old with me on the plane. I didn't want to slug back a shot of alcohol either, for the same reason. So I was left to take a flight to Indianapolis straight up, no sweet elixir to dull the fear of takeoff and landing, even if the entire flight took fifty minutes. All in all, I handled the situation fairly well; Kennedy kept me occupied with her little comments, funny as a standup routine, noticing everything from how my face looked like the bad ending to a story (her words) to how the toilet smelled undeniably rotten, like a grandpa had just been in there, she said. With all the one-liners she was spieling forth, I didn't have time to let my nerves get the best of me; still, I wasn't confused. When we landed I remained edgy, keyed up, and slightly sick to my stomach. I just thought it was the flight.

We stood in line at the Avis counter for twenty minutes or so before being shuttled to a deep, wide parking lot, jam-packed with enormous vehicles I'd opted to decline. Instead, we drove an economy car to Wabash, my luminous hometown, just under an hour and a half north. Kennedy had battled sleep on the plane and succumbed once I drove onto 465, the bypass from my youth that Third-Person Mother claimed killed more people each year than most of the really good serial killers freely roaming the streets of Indy. As Kennedy snored and the car rambled over the poorly kept pavement, seams in the road thump-thumping every second or two, I realized I was moving into a state of considerable anxiety. I hadn't been back to see my parents in nearly two years and hadn't been in Indiana during the summer for almost eight. In the end, I accepted my fear. I was scared to talk to my family about the book, scared to bring up certain details I thought I should share with them.

In my head, I planned out how I would discuss it with them in a roundtable fashion, the nuances of memoir as a literary form, maybe even read a few lines I thought had turned out particularly well. But even as I tried to imagine these scenarios I aborted them. True, some of the family had read my shorter pieces, both fiction and essays, but I'd never had any face-to-face talks with them about how much I loved writing, how for the life of me I couldn't understand to what extent I would've been ruined and torn apart had I not gotten the chance to use words to tell stories. By Elwood, Indiana, I decided I'd just have to choke down the fear and get on with it. The flat fields, ripe with corn and beans, stretched to clumps of trees perfectly visible miles and miles away. It was the sight of that landscape, so familiar and simple, that caused in me the desire to rush on to Wabash. In twenty minutes we were there, pulling up into the yard at my parents' house.

When we were teenagers Darren and I used to pose my mother's yard menagerie in disgusting stances. The deer would be humping squirrels twice their size, while the flamingos and geese engaged in hellish carnality. It was an awful thing to do, but we had a blast doing it. Sometimes she would say, after having been outside in the yard, "I just don't know how those figurines get into such odd postures." She'd dust off her coat and walk to the sink with a handful of dying flowers, a serious, placid expression on her soft face. "Looks to me like the wind did it, I guess." We'd be doubled over, hooting out laughter, while she,

oblivious to our juvenile pranks, placed the bunch of wild holly-
hocks, jute rope around their stems, into a mason jar.

Kennedy had wanted to surprise her grandparents, uncles and
aunts, and cousins, but in the end we thought we'd better 'fess
up and tell them about our planned visit. I knew it would please
my mother, but I also was well aware that it would provide her
with time to prepare some type of homecoming event, which
terrified me. Over the last year or so she'd come to be one of my
biggest fans. She'd asked for copies of the magazines and jour-
nals I'd published in and had gone to telling people about them.
I was happy she was proud enough to gossip about my writing,
but I was afraid she was going to write to the paper and have them
waiting to do a story on it. Or that she'd want me to visit people
I didn't know anymore to show me off, perhaps a handcrafted
shirt to mark the occasion. In my wildest fear-laden fantasies, I
pictured her enrolling me in the Canal Days Parade. I saw the
headlines in my mind: *Thirty-Something Crandell Boy Returns
Home for Parade, Wears an Updated Version of His 1976 Jumpsuit, Rides Children's Bike While Signing Copies of an Obscure
Literary Magazine!*

Seeing my mother for the first time in a couple of years, I
was taken aback by her teeth. She'd only had the one set of false
teeth since I was in grade school, and I had become accustomed
to them. They made her face. As far as I was concerned they were
real; I had trouble remembering what her original ones had looked
like. If I focused enough I could remember them, but for the
most part her false teeth, the first set, were the ones I'd always
known. The new teeth looked too long; they filled her mouth
with seamless white; the bridgework caused the space above her
top lip to fill in, making her smile look textbook and flawless. I
wasn't used to it. I liked her other teeth better; they were a part
of her.

She met us on the front porch. My sister Dana's little girl was with her. Jessica had been born prematurely; in one photo all of her little fingers fit on my sister's thumb. She's petite and pale, with a mop of curly hair. She reminded me quite a bit of Kennedy as the four of us sat down in the rocking chairs to listen to the collection of windchimes that hung over the eaves. It was late afternoon, muggy and sunny. My mother seemed unsure of herself, preoccupied with something. After a few minutes we decided to go eat, a merciful breeze gently cooling off the humid conditions as we climbed into the rental car. The girls sat in the back, free of the explosive air bags, while I drove and my mother reclined in the passenger seat. I backed the car out of the yard as she clicked her seat belt into place. I looked over my shoulder and instructed the girls to do the same. My mother cleared her throat and said, "You're gonna interview me, right?"

"Yes, Doris," I said. She hates when I call her by her first name instead of mother; she demonstrated it by mocking me, repeating my line before she told me, "Good, I want to talk to you."

I slept in a recliner the first night at the house in Wabash. I'd revisited the courthouse to view the lightbulb. I thought it would look small as an adult, but the thing is still monstrous, worth a peek if you ever get the chance. Kennedy had reluctantly gone with me after I picked her up from my sister's house, where she was helping care for the fifteen or so babies in the day-care center Dana operates out of her home. Kennedy had taught a few of the kids some sign language and hadn't wanted to leave with me for lunch and a trip to the courthouse to take in the glass case that was part of my history. We ate lunch at a little diner and took some pictures in town before I took her back to my sister's to finish up the day feeding and changing babies. She loved it.

The next day I spent almost the entire time at the library and didn't see my mother until dinnertime. She remained distant and somewhat awkward around me. We took ice cream to my dad at the county building where he worked a late shift for the transportation department, answering phones and doing light cleaning. After the ceiling tile factory had closed, a couple of years before his retirement age, he took the county job to survive. The place reeked of oil and diesel fuel as we ate ice-cream cones and sat in the office of the garage building. We talked briefly while the kids played around the desk. Before long, my sister took her kids and Kennedy back to her house for a sleepover, and I was left to drive my mother home. It was almost ten P.M. when we got back to the house. My mother fiddled around with some dishes in the sink as I set up the recorder. We didn't talk about it in the car, but once we were home, just the two of us, I miked her and opened a black leather-bound journal to ask her questions. I wanted to know about her hysterectomy, about how she'd suffered from it; it was the part of the story I couldn't get from memory. I had to have her tell me about the awful event.

We sat across a pine table from each other, a bowl of glass fruit between us. Sparkling grapes and green apples, sunny lemons and carroty oranges gleamed under the fluorescent light dancing weakly above our heads. I did a test on the tape, warming myself up, also giving her a moment to engage, but it didn't work. Both of us remained unnerved, tense at the thought of recording the questions of a son to a mother.

For some reason, I guess to combat my own nervousness, I began showing her my scrawled notes in the back of the journal. We'd talked over ten times on the phone about the book during the last six months, and somehow I thought if I shared my notes of those late-night conversations, phoning her from Atlanta to discuss some fragment of a memory, to nail down a date or specific event, it would prove to her how I didn't want to harm her, how I'd tried my best to get it right. On the tape I sound phony, pretending to be a reporter; I've kept it only for what she has to say.

My first question was, "So, to the best of your recollection, what do you remember about your hysterectomy?"

"Well," she said, her head down, hands before her on the table as if in confession, "they didn't tell me, you see." She picked up a pencil and began doodling on a scrap of paper. "They didn't. When I came to and woke up they told me, said they cleaned it out because it was infected."

I was taken aback by how she called her reproductive organs "it." At that table, the sink dripping water, the wind chimes out front gingerly tinkling, I looked at her face for the first time in a long time, I mean really looked at it. She'd gotten old on me. Her eyes behind bifocals were still big, brown ovals, eyes she'd passed on to all of us, but there was a distinct change in them. She was resigned, content, I guess. During my childhood I'd gotten used to their wildness, how she always seemed to be trying to figure something out, eyes wide and intense, burning with thought. Now, they seemed at ease. It was then that I discovered she'd actually been *waiting* to talk with me. Eager. I'd misread her uncertainty with me over the last two days. She'd been antsy to speak on tape, not reluctant, not dreading it like I'd thought. Over the next two hours she talked as openly as I could've hoped, filling in her own story as I told her about my memories. At times I thought her words would hurt me so much I'd never be able to write the rest of the book, but, in her typical style, she helped me create the truth. Like it was a parade outfit or a decorated room, she cut and pieced together her life from the fabric bolt of the past, putting it together with determination and hope, even a flair for exotic detail.

Near the end of our interview she told me about a doctor's visit she'd had only a year and a half ago.

"I am afraid of doctors. After they didn't tell me about that operation, I've always hated going. They ignored my emotions, told me it was just the woman in me." She took a sip of water from a clear glass, her eyes darting over the rim. She set it down and continued.

"I found a doctor who would sit down and listen to me. I went to Dr. Beejus in North Judson and the first thing he said was, 'Tell me your story. I want to hear it in your words.' He let me talk for forty-five minutes. He sat back in his chair and let me talk about myself. I told him all about the hysterectomy and not having hormones. I felt good with him. Someone finally listened to me. It took twenty-five years but I finally found a doctor who would listen.

"I told him my nerves were always on edge, that I couldn't let go of things in my head to get to sleep. He took all my history down. After a long while he sat up in his chair and said, 'Well, this all goes back to not having any treatment after your hysterectomy.' " She took a deep breath and looked down at her hands; they'd not really moved the entire two hours. It was getting late. Outside, a few cars accelerated by, exhausts rattling. The chimes had stopped making music. The night was still and warm.

She scribbled on a piece of paper. She seemed very tired. I'd asked her to recall some harsh events and she'd performed like a trouper. I'd asked her to re-create her reproductive history, such a clinical term for what I really had been interviewing her about. In reality, I'd coaxed her into confessing things she's kept locked up for years. And she'd done it for me because I was her child. Most of those confessions will die with me; some have shown up here.

I went to sleep on the couch in the living room while she waited for my father to come home after midnight. I heard him come in, the two of them mumbling back and forth, trying not to wake me. It was their soft conversation, hushed and continual, that lulled me to sleep. Before drifting off, I realized that in two months they'd celebrate their forty-fifth wedding anniversary. That number bounced around in my head along with their purring conversation. They sounded like they were still making plans, still figuring out what lay before them, and part of me was jealous, but mostly I felt happy, glad that they'd never really given up.

It was sunny and hot on our final day in Wabash. We'd all planned to meet at my sister's house for a late lunch of roasted ham, chips, and a huge assortment of fresh produce. Dana had purchased a cake that read: Redneck Reunion. Kennedy asked if she was a redneck. I told her no, none of us were, no one is. We milled around for a bit before someone suggested we get out the basketballs and start up a game. Only in Indiana do households have on hand enough basketballs for such an extended family. At one point, ten balls were flying toward the hoop. Before long, teams were divvied up and the games began. Derrick was impossible to guard. He drove the baseline, posted up like a wedge of cement, and shot banks until guarding him seemed only to make the points come more rapidly. Darren and I teamed up once, then we were divided; he was quick and cagey. As a kid, he'd dribble in one spot for what seemed like five minutes at a time, now though, being the lightest of us all, he played with the energy of a field rabbit. Soon the kids were getting bored with our extended play, so we got them on bikes and chaperoned their daredevil antics in a school parking lot directly behind the house. We ate and drank beer. The kids traced the outlines of their bodies on the asphalt. Derrick and his family had to get on the road. They were due back in Missouri by Monday afternoon, and had to stop by a few places before making the trip back. It was around six o'clock by now. My mother ushered us all to the front of the house for a picture.

We looked at old pictures at my parents' house earlier in the trip, finding horrible shots of graduations, first dates, farm implements, the river, cattle, field trips, Dina's surgery, my finger soakings, Darren's FFA accomplishments, the Terre Haute family, and my dad's parents in the nursing home. In one photo was a whole group of Crandells. It was a picture of my Grandpa Fred's family. On the back it listed Terrence Crandell, Dan and Sam Crandell, and a man named Captain Samuel Marksbury Crandell. He had supposedly killed his wife for cheating, and served during the Civil War. After the murder, he was asked by the state of Kentucky to head north. That meant Indiana. I stared at the picture. He would be my great-great-grandfather. They were a tough-looking group, plump and dark-eyed, rigid as they posed for a photo made from a strange box in front of them.

As we lined up in front of an old wagon wheel for the photo, the sun in our eyes, I recalled the picture of the other Crandells and tried my best to connect the bloodlines. Perhaps your last name is Crandell, or it might be spelled Crandall, Crandel, Crandle, or some other derivative. If so, know that this is only a start. I've recorded just a few months of my family in the midst of the late 1970s. There's still a lot of work to be done. I've tried my best to tell our story, but it's only a piece of it. If you look porcine or have a tendency to overeat, maybe we're related. If you've pursued a dream and fallen short, we might be kin. Write it down, tell some more of the story, because they're all the same, one connects to the other, directs us back as it moves the clan forward.

To be sure, we've been harsh on one another, sometimes even cruel. For whatever reason, the 7 D's have hurt each other, maimed one another, been ruthless at times with our love, but always protective when it comes to outsiders trying to hurt one of us. We could do it to each other, but it stopped there. As I look at both of the photos, the antebellum Crandells and the modern ones, I see something similar in their eyes. On average, people in my family weigh about 210 pounds. I want to make sure one thing is clear. There's a whole new litter of Crandells. My parents' 5 D's have reproduced. Like our forebears we can be fierce. Here's a list of the newest Crandells: Kennedy (mine), Nicole and Katlyn (Derrick's), Madison (Darren's), Casey and Jessica (Dana's). Dina doesn't have children but her nephews and nieces love her dearly because most of them are about her height. In any case, take heed. Don't screw with these babies. If you're a middle-aged mother in northern Indiana and you have a son who's a punk, don't let him date our girls. I mean, really, do you want to look out your picture window some night and see my people staring back at you, a total mass of nearly 1,500 pounds bearing down on your home because your son decided to get fresh with one of the Crandell girls? No, of course not. You don't want this family staring in at you, their noses slightly upturned, oinking, about to descend on your skinny suburban son. Remember, pigs are carnivores; they can and *will* eat anything. Just tell him to move on.

That night, the last one in Wabash, Darren and I took the kids to stay in the Holiday Inn Express just off Highway 24. It was no more than half a mile from our parents' house, but the kids wanted to swim and get silly in a rented room. We played in the pool and enjoyed the hot tub. My dad came by and put his bad knees in the hot water. It was hard to hear in the steamy room, but we talked about the kids and how much they'd grown. He started to get sleepy and left to go back to the house.

Up in the room, we asked for a rollaway bed. Darren slipped out to buy snacks while I supervised the kids in choosing an appropriate TV show, which wasn't anywhere to be found. We played a few games while we waited for Darren to return. In the end, they all fell asleep pretty quickly, tired from the long day, the pool, and from growing. Kennedy snored in her bed as I lay beside her. Darren came back and I shushed him before he could even speak. He smiled and I felt happy to be with him.

We drank a couple of beers he'd bought and chatted a bit. He went to the window and opened it. I was surprised it wasn't bolted shut. We were three floors above a large field of tasseling corn. To the left we could see the highway but the rest of the view was corn, a full moon lighting it up. Darren went to the bathroom to shower. The next morning he would hug me and say good-bye. Kennedy and I would fly back to Atlanta while he drove home to Roanoke, Indiana. I'd wanted to say thank you to him for taking such good care of me that summer of '76, for reading to me and helping me along, but I chickened out. Instead, I stood at the window, the shower humming in the back of the room, and looked at a house across the field. I could see the lights come on inside. Someone was up late, maybe making a sandwich in the town where light was born. I turned and went to each of the kids to make sure they had covers on. My parents' dream had not come true, the one about having their own farm, but they'd made another one work. They'd had a family, one that had gone on to do the same. In the end, in America, it's the only dream left worth having. I am the pig boy. I nursed from a sow, admitting it now feels like the right thing to do.

ACKNOWLEDGMENTS

I am deeply grateful to the following people for their wisdom, guidance, and support: Bob Mecoy, my agent and tenacious advocate; Cynthia Sherry, a kind and patient editor; and Sy Safransky and Andrew Snee at *The Sun,* for publishing a portion of this book in their wonderful magazine.

I am especially thankful for the generous support of the following groups that helped me pay the bills while writing: the Sherwood Anderson Foundation; the River City/Hohenberg Foundation; my considerate friends at Glimmer Train, Linda and Susan; and *Smithsonian* magazine.

My many thanks to Nancy Brooks-Lane for her love and encouragement and for laughing with me in all the right places. I would have never taken the leap to learn to write if it hadn't been for her support.

Last, my most heartfelt gratitude goes out to Derrick, Darren, Dina, Dana, Dan, and Doris for their fierce and unabashed love and familial strength. And finally, to my daughter, Kennedy, who helps me fly and who will someday take up this story and tell more of it. Her love means everything.